MW00713446

The DIY Musician's Radio Handbook:

How To Growth Hack Your Audience Building Using Indie Radio Airplay

By D Grant Smith

The DIY Musician's Radio Handbook:

How To Growth Hack Your Audience Growth Using Indie Radio Airplay

Written and Arranged By D Grant Smith

Cover designed by Philip Miranda

Copyright © 2016

All references to The Appetizer and The Appetizer Radio Show are used with permission from The Appetizer Enterprises, LLC.

Quotes and references sourced where indicated

**Since you picked up this book, you get a discount on The Indie Radio Promotion Course. Get your discounted link in the Introduction section

Published by
Clear Fork Publishing
P.O. Box 870
102 S. Swenson
Stamford, Texas 79553
Phone: (325)773-5550
Fax: (325)773-5551
clearforkpublishing.com

Printed and Bound in the United States of America.

ISBN - 978-0-9974370-0-3
Library of Congress - 2016937104

Dedication

No work is the result of just one person with a good idea. My life, work, successes and this book are the result of several people who have spurred me onward over the years, continued to believe in me and helped me take my work a step further along the path each and every bend in the road. Thank you!

This book is the result of a lot of encouragement, questions, and help from people who have inspired and led me along the way. A big thanks to:

My wife Leilani for believing in big dreams, your constant encouragement and love that goes beyond anything I know
My Mom, Dad, sister Emily, Rob and Kathy for the support, faith, and life-lessons that have made sticking to big goals doable

Close friends, mentors and real life networkers who live out the principles talked about in this book like Myra Dean, Steve Palfreyman, Larry Sabin, and Bird Thomas. You are an inspiration to me.

Table Of Contents

Introduction

Hello, my friend.

You are on a journey in growing your audience via indie radio airplay and digital promotion that has tremendous benefits for your music career. If you've tried doing radio promotion on your own and reached a dead end, you're not alone. That's the tale most artists experience. But I have good news for you.

You're now going to learn how to gain stations who play your music. You will also learn some very beneficial methods of growing your network and increasing your fan base by connecting with influential media professionals. What I'm going to show you in this book is the equivalent of Growth Hacking radio airplay.

The big secret isn't really a secret. It's just a mindshift change.

You're going to get your music heard on the radio, grow your fan base, and make your music more marketable. All of these things lead to success for you. They also lead to new opportunities to grow your audience powerfully by connecting with the **right people** for your fan base, not just anybody.

Since you're taking the right step forward to grow your music effectively, I want to give you even more to help with this process. This Radio Handbook is a part of an online teaching course-The Indie Radio Promotion Course.

The course details all of the pieces of this text Handbook complete with videos, and additional bonus material. Since you picked up this Handbook, you get an exclusive special outlet to gain more insights into the course. Visit this link for a course rate just for you: *http://dgrantsmith. com/indieradiocourse-1handbookreaderdiscount25*

(Please don't give this link out because it's special for you as a book reader)

Let's get to the Pulses of Radio.
Here are a few benefits of radio airplay for your music:

1. Increased recognition by music lovers on you, your sound, your releases, your touring, and what makes your music act stand out.
2. Increased sales of your music online, in stores, and at shows.
3. More attention to your band, your music releases, and more attendance at your gigs/shows.
4. Better opportunities to play better gigs in front of the right kind of fans - the ones who support the music they love.

How do I know you're going to be heard on the radio?

You've opened this book and are curious enough about the process to want to make it happen.

Throughout this book I'm going to confront the way that many artists go about growing their music careers, and what they try to do with radio.

For easy reference: Most artists = The common way.

I'm also going to address the **uncommon route** and **uncommon artist**. My experience with musicians and with gaining success via radio airplay has come from doing things differently than what most people do. I'm going to show you a path forward to grow your audience with radio that is different than what most artists do. It has proven time and time again to be successful where the common route isn't.

That common path I mentioned is the easy and "short" road to growth. Some musicians message individuals hoping to get followed on social channels in ways that end up looking like spam. Many times artists do the same with media contacts including radio, bloggers, podcasters and e-magazines. They contact media with a Me-First/Me-Only message that offers little-to-nothing to the recipient media outlet to want to feature them. Or worse, they only send radio stations a song attachment in an email and call that a submission.

"Whenever you find yourself on the side of the majority, it is time to pause and reflect." Mark Twain, author

You know, I made the same mistake so it is something that can be fixed. When I was first trying to get my radio show syndicated, I sent blanket emails out. It didn't serve me very well. Blanket messages led to little or no response from contacted stations.

I had to shift my method to get the results I wanted. There's a reason why the Me-First/Me-Only message doesn't work very well.

Later in this handbook, I'll tell you my story on what I did to take a radio show on a small market station to become a syndicated program that radio stations in over 20 states carry each week. I'll reveal the shift I made to go from the common route to the uncommon one.

"To do something that you feel in your heart that's great, you need to make a lot of mistakes. Anything that's successful is a series of mistakes."— Billie Joe Armstrong, Green Day

Blanket, Me-First messaging is what the 99% of musicians do, meaning that the vast majority of artists do not know that there is more to radio promotion (and relationship networking) that serves them. Many artists don't see the big picture of what radio provides for their careers: a connection point to the right audience and the right presenters.

These connections serve your future in much greater

ways than just having a song spun on a station. We'll dive into the specifics of these ways later on as well.

This radio promotion handbook is about more than just getting your music on the air or on the radio. This is a handbook for how to network and build awesome connections with influential media creators that will transform your work into something that is followed, celebrated, and showcased.

There is a process that makes all of this work.

Once you go through the process and have your own experience, curtail these methods to meet your communication and networking style. This is the path I have gone on and what has worked for me in building my platform. Every step in here has been executed personally with great success.

The very BIG key thing to remember as you go through this handbook is that the real work you're doing through contacting media for radio airplay is **bridge building** and **networking**. When you make a real, reciprocal connection with a radio or media outlet, you've built a bridge. That radio platform playing your music builds new connections with new audiences. Bridge building is networking and relationship growth. These are the essential pieces of everything you do to grow and reach new levels of success.

There are other services who offer something similar to

what I'm presenting in this handbook. However, to access their service will involve a very high price tag. Some of these companies and professionals are worth the fee, and others are not. It can be tricky when deciding how to get your music out there on radio, which is why this handbook is perfect both for artists who are starting out and those who have been making music for a while, as well as for managers, promotion companies, and PR firms who work to grow artists' audience through radio airplay.

In the following pages, I'm going to tell you exactly what to do on your own to grow your fan base, sell more music, play better venues, and have more success with your music using radio airplay.

I'll show you exactly how to frame your messages, emails, and press kit materials to be noticed and listened to by radio managers and program directors. And if all of this still seems like too much and you want to pay someone else to do it for you, I'll tell you some individuals and companies that do the best job at radio promotion to get the results you're looking for. I'll tell you the people I network with for radio promotion for the programming I create every week on my radio show.

Starting out, you can easily do much of this on your own without hiring someone to promote you on radio.

However, there will be some costs. They include:

Your time
A little money
Patience

I mention these three things because technology and society have almost sent us backward in our inability to do some tasks. The ease of technology makes us have such a hard time understanding the concept of process. Process is where time and patience come in. Process is an essential part of everything we do in life. Process isn't instant. There isn't an app that makes the process of growth and cultivation instantaneous.
Should someone ever be able to invent such an app, and it work, they'll be a billionaire instantly.

I did mention that this process (and adapting to it) will cost you some money. Even if you do all of the promotion work on your own, you're going to have to spend a little money for your efforts to work best. Which brings up one other preliminary point:

Anything worth building and pursuing is also worth investing in. Or as Benjamin Franklin put it, *"An investment in knowledge always pays the best interest."*

Mr. Franklin's quote means that if you want to skate by relying only on your talent, you're going to spend a lot of time frustrated that things aren't going the way you hoped.

If you want to grow your music, reach new fans, play venues with more than 20-40 people showing up, and reach music fans to the point where they buy from you, you're going to have to invest time, energy, and money into this endeavor.

No business or project has reached any level of success relying solely on talent or luck that has stayed successful over time.

<u>A Little Insight Into My Story</u>

To give you a foundation for where all of the insights come from, let me tell you just a little about me and how I've come to embrace the process I'll show you in this handbook. I've been working in radio in some form or fashion since 1998.
My experience with radio stations covers the entire spectrum from on-air host (also called DJ in some circles), reporter, interviewer, producer, manager, program director, program creator and program host.

In 2003, I created a music variety program called <u>The Appetizer Radio Show</u> specifically to be able to showcase unknown and emerging musicians to a broader audience. In the years since it was born, The Appetizer Radio Show has been an integral part of the early success of several great indie artists and bands including Lindsay Katt, Kelley McRae, The Rocketboys, Elliott Park, William Fitzsimmons, Birds Over Arkansas, Jerzy Jung, and many many more.

I'm very passionate about music, which is why I work in radio and also help musicians through coaching and mentoring. One of the best ways to grow your audience is through radio airplay.

Yet some artists spin their wheels and don't move their music career forward, simply by not communicating clearly or approaching stations the right way.

I've been in the position of a radio decision-maker both as a program host as well as a station manager for over 15 years. I've received countless submissions for airplay from artists in every genre, many across the US and others around the world. Based on the way that the submission is made, it can be obvious whether the artist or band is of the quality of music that deserves to be promoted on radio.

Sometimes, however, you can stumble upon a great artist who surprises you with an incredible sound and songwriting.

Unfortunately, too often some talented artists fail to create the connections they need, and the artist's promotions or messaging comes across the same way that musicians with lesser-talent do. Getting lumped in with musicians who don't have your quality is a fate I don't wish on anyone, which is why I've composed this handbook for just you.

"Success is...knowing your purpose in life, growing to reach your maximum potential, and sowing seeds that benefit others." John C Maxwell, best-selling author

Each of the steps and elements listed here have been done successfully. Actually, I've given you my exact process and template that I used to syndicate The Appetizer Radio Show.

I didn't use a syndication service or promoter/agent, though I did look at quite a few of those professionals in this process. The method I describe here has helped me make great contacts with radio stations and build some solid networking connections.

Some of the "mistakes" I'll talk about here are actions and processes I made initially in the first year of my own syndication process that didn't produce great results. One thing I discovered over time was that mistakes can become valuable only if you learn from them. Maturity comes when you and I learn from what doesn't work and make a shift.

"I don't want to give advice to a 19-year-old, because I want a 19-year-old to make mistakes and learn from them. Make mistakes, make mistakes, make mistakes. Just make sure they're your mistakes."— Fiona Apple, songwriter/performer

Relationship building is at the core of everything described in this handbook. If you aren't committed to establishing, growing, and building relationships with people to grow your music project and career, then you need to pick a different line of work.

Everything you do will stem from the relationships you build. I'm going to show you how to communicate clearly and build the connections you need to get your music heard so that your audience can grow.

Here's a little extra something to keep in mind: If you're wanting to get your music picked up by a record label, management group or PR company, you need to have a solid network. All of those entities work best when they are working with a musician who has built a strong audience AND a solid network of contacts. This radio handbook will help you grow your network through strong relationship building.

Make sure you're ready to move on

1. What are the 3 costs to doing radio promotion on your own?

A).

B).

C).

2. What is at the core of everything that will be talked about in this handbook?

Source: The Way to Wealth: Ben Franklin on Money and Success

Forward: Good Stuff To Key In On & Not Skip

Books are designed to teach. You may have a different learning style than other people you know. You can look at the chapter titles and be tempted to skip to the area of the book that you don't know or haven't been successful with and go from there.

That may work for you sometimes, but I know you'll get more out of this experience if you follow the process. If you want to get a Cliff's Notes version of what to do in this process to gain success and try to fast-track growth, here's all you need:

1. Know your band/music identity
2. Know how you compare to other artists in your genre
3. Do research on stations who cater to your ideal audience
4. Listen to these stations and have an experience to talk about
5. Contact stations/programs you have experienced to get airplay
6. Keep offering something to radio that benefits stations' and their audience
7. Follow up and build stronger relationships with radio and audience

That's it. Pretty easy isn't it?

The thing you may be wondering is, "How do all of these steps work? How can I make sure I do each of these steps the best way to get the results I want?"

That's what this handbook is for. Let's get started.

I'm not a scientist, but I do know this:
Einstein's Theory of Relativity is a familiar equation.
$E=MC^2$

Do you know that this equation is a simplification? What Einstein did was take a series of equations, elements and figures and after working with them over a period of time, simplified it, and this is how we understand relativity now.

Einstein was also a musician, with violin as his chosen instrument. Music impacted the way he thought, processed data, and changed the world of science.

"I live my daydreams in music. I see my life in terms of music. I get most joy in life out of music." -Albert Einstein

What I'm going to show you here is a process that I used to grow and create connections with radio stations, influencers in the music industry, be heard, showcased, and celebrated. I'm going to show you this process so that you'll understand how you can take it and simplify it to meet your personality.

Just a few quick notes here before we really get started.

It's really REALLY important to get these 3 things at the outset and not skip ahead to what you think you need to get radio promotion. Trust me.

I. I will reference small business a few times in this handbook. Many artists and creative people are afraid of business stuff, terminology, and references to it.

Don't be afraid of business stuff.

Here's why:

As a musician, you are investing your time, creativity, money, and talents into your music with the hope of it returning to you with growth (at least with some monetary return). How is that not the same thing that a small business owner or entrepreneur faces with their endeavors? See yourself as an entrepreneur in music, and everything you do to grow will become so much easier, especially with audience growth and fan building.

II. Your attitude determines a lot. Check yourself and your attitude towards people (in general and specific to who you're reaching out to) before you start doing the hands-on stuff presented in this handbook.

Make sure you are wanting to build reciprocal bridges between people as you connect with radio stations.

Having a positive and good attitude will come across in your messaging and (surprisingly!) be a deciding factor in station's taking an interest in you. Failing to have a good attitude (or simply just being in it for only yourself) can come across instantly to others as someone to avoid. You don't want to turn people off from the outset by showcasing an attitude that is not in check.

III. This is a process. Each step is important. Follow the process laid out here to get the best results.Shortcuts rarely produce beneficial results for anyone.

To help showcase the power of process, and the unique aspects of going against the grain, I've incorporated some quotes from great thinkers, authors, entrepreneurs, performers and musicians along the way.

Winning the Golden Ticket or Taking The Magic Beans

There might be a magic pill you can take to get radio airplay, but I haven't found it. You know who else hasn't found it? Innumerable pop stars, major-label bands, and well-funded musicians out there trying to get their music on the radio and streamed on Pandora, Spotify, Mog, Apple Music, etc. Shortcuts to audience growth and financial success hasn't been achieved by the artists who are on major labels that have bottomless budgets to make that happen.

If big pocketbooks can't buy shortcuts to success with a simple formula, those of us in the DIY/unsigned/indie/entrepreneurial path can't either.

Platinum artists don't have a magic button that gets them accepted and praised by media or fans. Those who spend their time searching for a magic button to bring about success will find themselves wasting their time.

What I've set out here to do is chronicle the individual steps that it takes to do 2 big things for you as a creative and artistic individual:

1. Create relationship connections between you, the media (radio, online outlets, blogs, etc) and your audience (both current audience and potential ones).

2. Position your music to the best people (aka the right audience) who can connect you to more of your ideal audience.

This is a turnkey solution that many indie artists have used as well as effective, successful PR and radio promotion companies. This process is what successful people do to build real connections with influencers who care about the artist before they experience the art.

You may already have a list of station contacts and may already have successfully pitched your music to radio. If so, that's excellent!

Take the insights here and use them with what you already have. Knock your radio promotions out of the park. If you don't have a list of contacts yet, don't worry. We'll cover that towards the end.

Make sure you're ready to move on

1. What 3 things do you need to have in place before you start this process?
A).

B).

C).

2. Is there a secret or magic way to get your music instantly liked and praised by music fans around the world?

3. Who has successfully used this process of getting radio adds for indie and unsigned artists?

Section 1: An Overview Of Effective Radio Promotion

Part One: A Readiness Question

"Is radio airplay and promotion of music a waste of time for artists, especially those not on a label?"

It's a question I get asked a lot from artists who are just starting out as well as those who have had a few spins on some stations. The answer is simple: No. Radio airplay is one of the best ways to get your music heard by real music fans and not just streaming music listeners.

Radio airplay is also a great way to put your sound in front of potential fans to sell more music as well as get more attendance to your shows.

The kicker for gig/venue attendance and for more music selling is that your radio airplay needs to be targeted, meaning that you shouldn't try and get placement on just any station. There are a few quintessential elements to look for when you're reaching out to stations or programs for radio airplay. Knowing the format of the stations and programs you're marketing to is essential to getting the right radio airplay.

If you perform Americana music, it won't make a difference in the world to send out a song for submission to a hip-hop/R&B station.

There are a few companies and professionals in radio marketing who are really worth their salt and do fantastic work. However, there are several individuals and organizations who are in the radio promotion market who is the opposite. For you to know the difference between the people who claim to get your music heard (at a pretty significant fee), and those who actually deliver will save you countless hours, anxiety, and money.

In this handbook, I'm going to break down the essential elements involved in getting your music heard on the radio. I'll show you how to focus your attention on programs and stations that are geared towards your unique sound, style, and audience type. I will show you how you need to look for stations who have standards that they follow in their decision making, and how to set similar standards for yourself in promoting your music to get the best results.

You'll see questions asked throughout this book in italics. These are questions I get a lot from artists all the time. Instead of putting those questions in an FAQ, I've incorporated them into the flow of this handbook, organized in the sections where the answers are covered with details provided. If you have further questions after reading this, feel free to reach out to me directly. I've provided my email at the end of the book.

We'll also look at digital submissions versus physical CDs mailed out for submissions. There are some radio music programs and stations who only accept digital submissions and others who are the exact opposite. There are strong arguments for both methods, and I'll show you how to pick the best option for your particular needs and sound.

Together, we'll take it a step further as I'll give you some names of companies and individuals who do radio promotion really well. Though I'm in the market as a program host, radio promoters are different individuals. Radio promoters are the ones who get an artist's music out to stations for a fee and usually for a specified period of time only.

From my experience in radio, I have a list of strong contacts that I've worked with for over a decade who serve as decision-makers at their respective stations and programs. The insight provided here doesn't just come from my opinion and preferences when choosing music for airplay. My contacts and radio colleagues have shared their take on music submissions and the key elements they look for when playing new music. I'm speaking on behalf of program hosts, indie music stations, music blogs and media outlets who accept music submissions. These insights, based on what I've discussed with several colleagues and what I've learned in conferences featuring radio managers are the basis for what is presented here to help you build connections with people in this industry.

Finally, I'll show you the process that I take when selecting music for my program. It's similar to the process others have who do what I do as a host and/or indie music programmer for radio. This insight will give you the best perspective in knowing how you can position your music and your brand to get the most airplay and build strong connections with stations to air your music.

"Change is inevitable. Growth is optional." -John C Maxwell, best-selling author

This DIY path for radio promotion can save you a considerable amount of money and help you build some very strong personal relationships/connections for your music that will benefit you greatly.

Aside from money, the greatest cost you will experience doing things on your own is time. It will take time to send the messages and packages out, do the followup necessary to find out the status of potential airplay and update your contact list. But in the end, it is more than worth it to choose this road.

If you choose to hire a PR or radio promotion company (or individual) to get your music out to stations, you can save yourself a ton of time and potential anxiety by learning this process. However, most services in radio promotion (or marketing in any other way) come with a price tag. Sometimes the financial return on that investment is not as great or timely as expected.

However, if you pick the right company, your results will be more than worth it.

I'll give you my 2 cents on who is trustworthy and what types of companies to avoid later on.

Throughout this handbook, I'll tell you specifics that I've seen and used to help indie artists grow their music and their audience.

"If you help enough people get what they want, you will get what you want." – Zig Ziglar

This book is not intended for people who treat music like a hobby. The purpose of this is to teach you fundamental aspects to how radio airplay can be used to help boost your music career, how to avoid common mistakes bands make with radio promotion, and directly answer specific questions that have been asked to me by musicians, both as a radio program host and as an indie music coach/ mentor.

Those two perspectives play into how this handbook is laid out, the benefits that this has for you as an indie artist, and how you can use this handbook to increase your levels of success in music selling, touring, booking shows, and growing your fan base.

Part Two: Natural Station Selection

There may be only a handful of radio stations in your area (depending on what part of the country you live in),

but according to Hypebot, there are over 15,000 radio stations* in the US (not including the countless indie web radio stations in the States).
Can you imagine your music being featured on 15,000 radio stations in the US alone? If that were possible, it may seem very easy to grow a strong, vibrant and passionate audience for your music. Hell, you'd hardly have to do much touring or marketing with your music playing on every radio outlet in the US (but not for those living outside the States).

How feasible do you think this scenario is to get your music on 15,000 American stations in one swoop? Strangely, there are too many bands and artists who confuse the number of radio outlets available to mean that they should try and get their music on each and every one of them. That couldn't be further from the truth.

There are certain stations you should spend your time and energy connecting with, and others you should leave alone entirely.

For the purposes of this handbook, there are 2 main types of radio, commercial and non-commercial (nonprofit) stations. I'm going to be referencing only 1 type of radio station from here on out: non-commercial radio. Non-commercial radio falls into a few other categories including public and community radio, college stations, and indie web radio stations. Here's why this type of radio will be our focus:

Non-commercial and public radio stations are (mostly) non-profit organizations with a specific mission to serve their local community and/or the interests of people who support their specific programming.

Notice that I said specific programming. Your music has a specific sound, even if you are combining the styles of a few different genres within your overall sound. If you are playing a combination of bluegrass with an alt-rock vibe, a hip-hop radio station is not going to be a good fit for you.

There are artists every day who send us (referring to public radio and The Appetizer Radio Show) music submissions who don't fit the format of our radio show at all. The Appetizer is a variety program, meaning that we cover a fairly wide spectrum of musical styles. However, we don't play everything, and most stations with engaged audiences aren't playing everything either.

College stations may be the one exception, but they are particular to a point as well. Still, a college station may cover the gambit of programming styles, but they still have a particular audience who listens for particular styles of music. Particular does not mean everything.

"Why is the focus for this handbook on Non-commercial, public, indie and college radio?"

These are the stations who are NOT controlled by a corporation and who regularly play DIY, indie and unsigned musicians in their daily playlists and programs.

Also, because they aren't corporately owned, you as an indie/unsigned/DIY artist have a much greater chance to connect with the station management and staff. These stations and programs are also reaching the best audience for your music to be played. Do you know why?

Non-commercial, public, indie and college radio exist for the purpose of fulfilling particular programming needs within their communities that are not met by the corporate stations. When I say corporate stations, I'm referring to the mainstream FM and AM stations that are owned by Cumulus, Clear Channel, and other big business corporations. They mostly feature the same 20-30 artists all day long, replaying the same songs over and again, mixed with 5-8 minute spans of commercials for products most people aren't interested in.

NPR is one of the largest public radio broadcasting networks. To give you some perspective, here are some stats* from NPR regarding their audience size and engagement:

- On air, NPR reaches 26.2 million weekly listeners through more than 1,000 public radio stations. Online, NPR.org attracts a growing audience of 25.6 million unique monthly users.
- 87% of listeners consider NPR to be "personally important to them."
- 96% of listeners take action in response to something they heard on NPR.
- 76% of listeners discuss content with friends, family, and colleagues

NPR is a model for most public radio and indie stations. Their audience engagement is a reflection of the connection that non-commercial stations have with their audience each day.

This is significant when you think about the people who are listening to these radio stations. This type of engagement is what you as a musician want with your fan base. These are the potential fans for you to seek out.

The target demographic for commercial stations are people who just want to experience the ordinary same-old stuff. They like the trendy stations with the same handful of songs played all day every day. They want to reach people who either only like trendy, pop artists or who just want *something* to listen to in the background. The corporate radio station listener is usually not as loyal to the artists they claim to enjoy. Most commercial radio fans don't own a lot of music (digitally or in hard copy of CD/vinyl). These are not the individuals you want to reach.

On the contrary, you want to present your music to people who are engaged, passionate, and supportive of the artists they enjoy. Public and indie radio is where these people are tuning in to discover new music like yours. Their interest in finding great new music is what makes them loyal to the non-commercial stations they tune in to regularly.

Also, because these stations are mostly nonprofit, they rely on the financial support of their listener-base to operate. This means that their listeners have a vested interest in the quality of music they feature (they are discerning professionals who have standards for what they will play and what they won't).
These are most likely the types of people who will support your music when they listen and enjoy it, allowing you to grow your music in new ways.

An important point to note: NPR is not the only public or indie radio organization out there. Many web-based indie radio stations carry NPR, as well as American Public Media, BBC, PRI, and various independent producer programs (such as The Appetizer Radio Show). These stations have audiences with very similar dynamics as those who carry NPR programs and music shows.

You might be wondering how radio airplay can help you in a digital age? Great question. I'll show you in Chapter 1.

Make sure you're ready to move on.

What is the true purpose of radio promotion?

What types of radio stations should you reach out to and why?

Source: http://nationalpublicmedia.com/npr/audience/

Chapter 1: Maximizing The Benefits Of Radio Airplay

The initial question I asked to start this handbook was:

"Is radio airplay and promotion of music a waste of time for artists, especially those not on a label?"

I said that the answer is a resounding NO. I know and have experienced first hand the benefits of radio airplay for indie and DIY artists in nearly every genre of music. These benefits include stronger attendance at gigs and concerts, more song and album purchases (both online and at live shows), better booking opportunities, and even licensing for TV and film.

For all of this to work in your best interest, you need to broaden the perspective you have on what it is that you are trying to do with radio promotion.

Unless you're independently wealthy or have a stream of income not related to music that still allows you to have other hobbies or interests, you should be trying to make money (in some way) with your musical endeavors. That being said, the money you invest in your music needs to return to you in some form. This return can be greater exposure to new audiences, a more solid fan base, better buzz on your new releases, etc.

Radio airplay works best for you when it's a part of a broader plan to grow your music. If all you're trying to do is get plays, I'd have to ask you what your end goal is. I say this because I've talked with artists who can't see past getting their music played on a station or a streaming site. Soundcloud is a great resource for musicians, but even 100,000 streams doesn't benefit you unless those plays can be connected to something else.

Radio airplay is beneficial to you in a variety of ways. The key element, though, is where that airplay takes place, the audience of the platform your music is heard on, and the type of listener that the station draws in.

My advice to you is simple: Go the Indie/Public/Community Radio Route. Focus your radio submission activities on the non-commercial radio platforms to gain the attention and airplay you seek. Targeting both FM and web stations puts your music in front of a specific group of people who listen with intent. That intention is to discover new artists, to get better music programming, and to grow their music libraries.

As a music coach and mentor, my #1 focus when working with individual musicians is to grow your core audience group (aka your Super-Fans). Most music coaches reference this group of people as a key part to having a successful music career. I believe that music and business share this commonality, and I'll take it a step further.

It's quintessential to have a core group of fans who are passionate about your unique offering, regularly buy something from you and share their experiences with your music to their friends and contacts. It's grassroots, word-of-mouth marketing that comes from individuals like this that have turned some of the biggest names in business and music into powerhouses.

Public and Indie Radio is one of the best incubators for Super-Fans of music. The reasons are actually quite simple. Public and indie radio operate (usually) as nonprofit organizations. Nonprofits have legal restrictions placed on how they operate, what they can and cannot do, and how they can receive money from outside entities placed on them by the government that they must adhere to.

Unlike Pop stations (aka Commercial Radio), nonprofit stations who are on the FM dial can't sell advertisement. What this means is that they don't program hours of content with giant commercial breaks covering 5-8 minutes of time.

Nonprofits also rely heavily on individual contributors to fund their programming. This means that they ask the people who listen to them to give financially to keep their station on the air.

"This sounds like public and indie radio is a bunch of beggars who are constantly asking for donations or they will go off the air. I've heard those radio spots before, and it turns me off.

*Why would I want my music on those stations if they're just going to ask other people for money to play **my** music?"*

On the contrary, when a nonprofit asks for support they aren't begging, though it is understandable to associate begging with asking. Here's where the benefit is (and where your perspective shift will make a difference): stations who rely on the financial support of other individuals and businesses mean that they have a strong connection with their listenership.

When you give money to ensure something will live, your investment takes on a new meaning. Also, you don't give to something you don't personally (and passionately) believe in. Your Super-Fan is someone who is passionate about your music, to the point where they spend their money on you so you can keep presenting them with more music. Public and indie radio is supported by Super-Fans of their programming. You have a greater opportunity of gaining more of your core audience by being heard by people who are inherently passionate about the stations they are tuned in to.

Choosing this route to airplay puts your music in front of the **right** audience, the audience that is committed to great music and seeing it continue. Which leads to greater opportunities for your music to be searched for via online and streaming services like Pandora, Spotify, Soundcloud, Bandcamp, Reverbnation, Youtube and more.

There are an innumerable amount of artists with pages on the streaming platforms. Anyone who spends any amount of time on these platforms can hear a million artists from anywhere on earth. This volume of content can become overwhelming, which is why most strong fans of music are not using Reverbnation or Soundcloud for music discovery, though there is some of that taking place.

Your music streaming and broadcasting needs to be tied to a bigger-picture if you want to achieve greater success. A Bigger-Picture is a next-step journey past just getting airplay or streaming. When you can link your touring to a national radio campaign for your new album, you have a greater opportunity to play more sold-out venues or festivals. This marketing is what can lead to licensing opportunities with TV and film because your music is being experienced in greater quantities by different groups of people, which is one thing TV and film music directors are looking for.

"But I heard that even if my song gets played 1,000 times on one station, I could only get like $10 royalty out of that. Why should I try and get radio airplay when I could do the same thing on Pandora and actually make money?"

I'll admit to being critical of streaming services like Pandora and Spotify in the past, yet there are positive merits to both that benefit you as an artist. I'll elaborate on their pros and cons in a moment, but first I want to answer this question very directly.

Music airplay and streaming are not reliable sources of income for any artist in the long term, including those who have hit records and hit songs. The mainstream artists fluctuate on the royalties they receive from radio and from the Pandora/Spotify streaming outlets based on the number of spins/streams among other factors.

Depending on where you live (globally), and the amount of radio airplay you get, both radio and streaming royalties can provide a little bump in your pocketbook, but nothing to the tune of making you rich. If you want to get your music heard on the radio or streamed so that you can just chill and not do any work, you may want to find a financier or pick a different profession. Neither method is going to get you a lot of money from the airplay alone, which is why your music promotion through media (FM, web radio, and streaming services) has to be a part of a Bigger-Picture plan for you to achieve real success.

However, as of the time of this writing, most FM and web radio airplay have seen big changes in royalty payments to ASCAP, BMI, and Soundexchange. As of Feb 1, 2016, the web radio platform Live365 was shutdown due to the rate increase for small webcasters, who now have to pay the same rate that larger stations do. This push came from both the big stations and the major record labels in an effort to take competition away from the big artists.

In the end, it hurts you the DIY musician more because there are (potentially) much fewer stations available who are interested and willing to air your music.

However, there are still plenty of indie and public radio stations who are still following the rate rules for royalties and also open to playing music from indie, unsigned and DIY artists like you.

Radio airplay factors in a guessed-upon audience size based on the market of the station, its listener data, and other factors. Either way, it's assumed that if a song airs on a station, more than one person will hear it. This is not true with streaming services like Pandora or Spotify, even if the outlet where the music is heard is a club or venue with several people present. One play or stream on Pandora is treated as though one individual heard it. The payout, therefore, is much smaller on a per song/per stream basis.

When you have radio airplay, you have a greater opportunity to make the connections you need for your music to grow. This includes the relationships you cultivate with individuals who listen to these stations and then follow you on social media, the contacts you make from the station managers and hosts who play your music, the networking created from getting multiple station carries, and the potential for greater bookings for tours and festivals because of the increased media you are heard on. A strong press kit and management can help get the best bang for your buck when using your media exposure to open up new doors.

Make sure you're ready to move on.

1. Name 3 benefits from radio airplay:

A).

B).

C).

How does radio work with a broader plan to grow your music?

Chapter 2: The Interaction Radio Has With Pandora, Spotify, & Other Streaming Services

In the mid-2000s when Pandora first emerged in the digital realm as a means of hearing music without having to endure commercial breaks, much of the radio world balked. Even in public radio, the thought that individuals could have access to millions of songs at a time without a middleman or programmer to curate the selections caused many to become worried. This was one of the first problems I had with the service because music curation is an art and skill. To remove the curator from the equation, you rely on chance or (worse) some computer algorithm to tell you what sounds good.

Pandora has since modified itself in a few ways but along the path emerged a second similar service: Spotify. Spotify has become more used in some capacities because of the greater access to indie and unsigned artists than Pandora. Spotify also allows individual users to create their own playlists, which can seem like the removal of the music curator but it isn't. Curators with playlists that get shared often are revealed to be great at selecting quality music. To me, this is a better way to discover new artists and new music in the streaming universe.

Spotify does have a few problems when it comes to its relationship with the artists who submit their music. Taylor Swift's removal of her entire catalog in 2014 before the release of an album set off a firestorm of media looking into how fair the compensation was for artists who had millions of streams/plays. The results were not very promising for artists looking to make their streaming royalties a part of their revenue stream. For even artists like Swift, who had millions of streams on a daily basis, the payout to her was negligible.

Royalty payouts for artists are higher on the radio than it is for either of these services, for the reason mentioned in the previous chapter. Still, radio has a unique relationship with these two competitors, and not all of it is negative. Once again I'm mentioning Pandora and Spotify. There are several other streaming platforms that are similar in this way.

One of the correlations that radio shares with both Pandora and Spotify is the bar set for what gets heard. There are exceptions to this, mostly with small indie and web radio stations, but the production quality and songwriting level for what is posted on Pandora/Spotify and what airs on the radio are both high. I'm not saying that every song on any of these platforms is inherently excellent or worth listening to. I am saying that songs that get any traction are those that have been produced well and have the compositional integrity to create connections with listeners.

Not every song that is heard on the radio is going to make traction with listeners. Some songs are duds, and they still get airplay due to the interests of the programmer, or worse, some financial incentive for the broadcaster to play the music. Here is where radio promotion should be looked at very scrupulously.

Early on I pointed out that there are credible and professional radio promotion services who do a great job of making connections with stations and use those relationships to get music adds. Other promoters use greenbacks to get artists heard. This method is not only unethical and illegal but also frowned upon by the individuals you want to connect with, especially music directors for TV and film.

Music review sites run this gamble too with the potential for paid reviews given to support an artist or album. Amazon and iTunes are both subject to this kind of false support, where someone with an account can give a 5-star review for an album that isn't worth its weight in bubbles. Whereas Pandora and Spotify are more driven by individual response to music, where the listeners have a direct hand in the promotion and ongoing airing of songs, you can't pay for others to play your music on a rotation.

At best, one could pay for playlists to be created and shared on Spotify, but this runs some big risks with offending and upsetting users, and certainly shouldn't be done for promotion.

Radio and the streaming platforms are also driven by numbers, where the interest and support of individual musicians create opportunities for growth for the artist. The more your music is played, the greater your audience reach is (potentially).

Make sure you're ready to move on

1. What relationship does radio have with Pandora and Spotify?

2. What do you need to do to make sure your music is ready to be liked and shared on streaming services like Pandora and Spotify from what you know about radio airplay?

Chapter 3: Getting Your Music Radio-Ready

Not every band is ready to be on the radio. The same is true for bands who want to submit music for spins on Spotify, Pandora, or other digital distribution outlets. There are several reasons why a band or artist is not acceptable for radio airplay, and the reasons have more to do with development than talent or sound.

It's vital for your short-term and long-term success to vet your sound and your production to make sure it's of the quality for radio airplay before you officially begin the process of putting yourself out there. You can spend countless hours, dollars, emotional and physical energy working to promote a product that isn't ready for mass distribution. Regardless of the techniques used to market yourself, if your music (product) isn't of the quality for radio airplay, it's going to be a tough road for you.

How can you know if your music is ready for radio?

I don't get this question as often as perhaps I should, and neither do most radio station managers or directors. It's a sad thing to listen to an artist who has a good heart and some discernible musical talent, but for one reason (or several) the music isn't radio worthy yet.

Here are three key metrics that make a song (or recording) radio worthy, from the perspective of multiple radio station managers and program hosts (yes, I checked with multiple people to verify what the industry is looking for):

1. Good sound production quality
2. Good songwriting
3. An enjoyable listening experience

Sound Production Quality-There is music that is heard on the radio from some very prominent names where the sound quality isn't top shelf. This only happens in very select instances, usually when a basement tape recording is released or some demo version that was previously lost. Only in these instances is it permissible for the quality of the recording to not be a prerequisite for airplay. One reason for this is that the artist is already a household name, and thus has earned the right to not have to have gone to the studio and shelled out the track. Also, when Bob Dylan releases a taped song that was recorded on Beta in a small space, even modern technology can only modify it to a certain extent.

Make sure that the recording you are sending to a station or media outlet is the highest grade possible with your budget or with the production abilities you have.

Does this mean that you must go into a recording studio to get your music produced in order to get radio airplay? Not necessarily.

Some of the artists I first discovered for The Appetizer Radio Show years ago, who have gone on to perform with Lady Gaga and sell out world tours, first sent me music that was recorded in a New York apartment or their basement in a small town in IL.

Here is one thing that 21st-century technology does provide from a recording and production end: you can aquire excellent equipment and gear to record yourself at a high-quality level using your living room or apartment as recording space. It hasn't been historically possible for musicians to create the quality recordings in decades past that it is today.

Have a producer listen to your music and give you some feedback on the sound. It's important that the producer or music professional be someone you trust for honest feedback and not necessarily someone who might try to use that situation to get you into their studio to sell you on a multi-thousand dollar recording project. I've used some select producers through Fiverr.com to refer musicians to for help in this realm (particularly with recording on their own). If you want to know if your sound quality is radio-worthy, send me an email or reach out through my site, and I can give you some feedback.

Sound quality is paramount because radio is an all-audio medium. Even if the performers are the best-looking people on earth or the most talented performers at their instrument, without a quality sound they don't have anything of value to offer radio.

Radio program hosts and managers alike get countless artists who email and snail mail music that is of poor sound quality. If you don't put a value on your sound quality, you come across as an amateur and won't be taken seriously.

Songwriting-Your songs need to be appealing to the songwriting elements. Songwriting is more than just lyrics and prose. Songwriting also includes the instrumentation, composition, and arrangement of the song. If all of your songs have the exact same song structure, you lack songwriting talent. This is more than just knowing more chords on a guitar or playing different iterations of chords in a sequence. There are many different ways to modify your songwriting from a composition and arrangement standpoint, but if someone were to listen to 2 of your songs and they sound so similar that you can't tell them apart, you need improvement in your songwriting.

"... but I believe that music can change a life, because it changed mine." — Charlotte Eriksson, writer; poet; songwriter

Love songs are one of the most common forms of songwriting. We've had recorded music for nearly a century. In all this time, there have been hundreds of thousands of songwriters who have written about love sought and love lost. This means we have heard a billion ways to say "I love you; you're beautiful; be mine" through song and lyric.

If you write love songs, come up with something that

hasn't been said (or sung) before. This is one element of songwriting from a lyrical standpoint that keeps artists from crossing the threshold into radio airplay. If your songwriting sounds bland or monotonous, you're not going to offer radio something new to put out there for an audience to grab ahold of.

Enjoyable Listening Experience- When you hear a song that you like, it's an enjoyable experience. However, it's not always easy to instantly qualify what specifically it is about a song that you enjoy. Sometimes it's just the hook or chorus that's appealing, and that's the reason. The song could have a cool guitar or drum solo or the vocalist could have a great range. The song could tell a story that captures your imagination and pulls you in.

The subject matter may tie into something you've experienced that creates an emotional connection because you have never been able to express the feelings the way the song did. All of these are enjoyable experiences created from listening to a song. Yet, there are other descriptions of enjoyable listening experiences. This piece of the puzzle is what every song should do for the listener that hears it on the radio.

An enjoyable listening experience is the mission of the radio station. It's what keeps people listening to that station instead of changing the station to search for something else to listen to. Stations want to keep their listeners attached to their station.

We all know that we live in a world of infinite choices, available every nanosecond of the day, making listener retention one of the most difficult and also sought out aspects of radio programming.

If your song doesn't create an enjoyable experience by listening to it, you're not giving a station a reason to play it because they would be going against their mission and their business plan by airing your music.

When you can nail all three of these elements, you have something that is Radio-Ready. How can you know if your sound quality, songwriting, and listener experience is really up to the test? I work with individual songwriters and musicians regularly just on these 3 elements. If you'd like some help or even some double checking to see where you are, contact me for help. You can also contact some individual indie music bloggers and writers to give your music a try. Their feedback may shine some light and provide some insight if you are ready for a more mass-audience approach to promoting your music.

Make sure you're ready to move on

1. Is your music is Radio-Ready? Why or why not? How can you tell if it is?

2. What 3 key elements are radio programmers and music show hosts looking for when choosing new songs and bands to feature?

3. Why are these 3 elements important for you to grow your music?

A).

B).

C).

Chapter 4: Essential Ingredients To Radio Promotion

Essential Ingredients To Radio Promotion include:
1. Knowing your brand/sound identity
2. Having the right station list
3. Contact promotion done properly
4. Knowing your offer

Before we dive into the key components of radio promotion and how it works, let's take a more broad perspective on the overall use of music in media.

Radio doesn't have the same role in the promotion of music and entertainment of people that it used to. There was a time when radio was the premier entertainment vessel (outside of live events). You've probably seen the movie A Christmas Story, where a little boy in the 1950s wants only a Red Rider BB gun for Christmas and stops at nothing to get this. In this movie, the boy stops everything he's doing when his favorite radio program, Little Orphan Annie, comes on the air. This was the way America experienced audio entertainment for several decades.

The advent of TV changed radio's dominance as a form of media, but it wasn't affected in the realm of exposing audiences to the newest music acts.

TV would eventually make a mark on the music scene in the 90s with the birth of MTV, which first aired music videos and not the reality TV shows they do these days. The 90s also saw the advent of a new kind of radio-public and community stations (which actually were birthed in the 1970s and 1980s but really caught on in the 90s). These stations were predominantly non-profit in organization and served the communities where the signal broadcasted with unique programming in the arts, news, and other entertainment.

As the Internet was born and began to take new holds in communication, web radio emerged in the late 1990s as a means for different types of programming to be broadcast around the world, all from one location. Terrestrial (FM) radio did not have that capability and still doesn't. Web radio continues to expand, and several large corporations have gone into the world of web broadcasting to broaden their audiences by offering unique forms of music engagement. Apple, Sony Music, Sirius FM, and Google all have their hands in the web radio/media universe of music programming.

Which brings us back to where radio fits into all of the marketing, promotion and growth potential for emerging DIY and indie musicians today. Radio might not be the only method for artists to get their music out to the world, but choosing the RIGHT radio platforms to be heard can make a dramatic difference in the growth and longevity of your music.

Radio continues to be one of the best ways that emerging bands go from being regionally known to booking national and world tours, playing on stage with late night TV shows, licensing deals on TV and film and more.

The first ingredient to focus your attention on has to do more with your sound than that of the radio station, regardless of whether it's FM or web radio. If your music doesn't just fit in one genre, determine 3 styles of music that you could use to define it. If you are a 4 piece band with acoustic guitars in the style of folk or singer-songwriter, but your drums and bass are more aggressive, and your vocals dive into realms of jazz and pop, you have a dynamic sound that fits into the folk rock, AAA, and indie rock styles. All three of these categories are fairly broad, but it gives you a reference point for when you start looking at stations to market to.

For artists who don't have any radio carriage yet and are just starting this process, look for web radio channels who fit your musical style and spend some time looking at their websites, read up on how they are presenting music, and see what their music submission rules are. This is a very important part of the process, and though it may take a little time, will be well worth it as you gain stations.

I would avoid stations and platforms that "accept everything," meaning that they don't have a process for music submission and all you have to do is send them your music without any qualifiers. Music fans are picky, and you should be too.

Radio programmers are picky on what they will air, so it makes sense to be selective of where you send your music to. Those outlets who will "play anything" are not selective, and chances are their audience isn't as engaged as those who are.

There are a few reasons to avoid these "accept everything" channels, even if you're just starting out and want to get your first few radio spins. Here is why I would avoid them:

1. Stations/Channels who accept everything don't have criteria for what is good and what isn't, meaning that their audience isn't necessarily as engaged or they aren't programming for quality. If anything is permissible, what does that say for the quality and excellence of your music? Especially if you could be aired in the same set as musicians who lack talent, quality production, or songwriting worth listening to.
2. If a station just has a portal for submissions, they rarely take the time to notify you on when your song aired (if it does) or what the status of the rotation is. They might not even have access to that information, which doesn't serve you.
3. They probably don't report their content data to the appropriate services like Soundexchange or ASCAP/BMI, which help regulate any potential royalties you may receive from airplay.
4. The listenership of the station may not be an engaged audience who values quality music, and the listenership may be so widespread that it is of little

benefit to you (i.e. the station is based in Atlantic City, but the audience is primarily in India, South America, and a few folks in Asia who may not understand or truly connect with your music).

There are several individuals and organizations who market musicians and music to radio that treat their clients as though the stations or contacts have no submission standards. Avoid these people at all costs, because they do a disservice to the musicians paying them to market their music to radio. Their Email music submission messages look like this:

Subject Line: XYZ Band Release Drops
Today For Adds on Radio
Message Text: Artist: (Artist Name)
Song: (Song Name)
Label: (Label)
-MP3 Song file attached-

I'm telling you the truth here. Yes, there are individuals who have convinced some artists that they will get radio airplay through this kind of messaging and communication.

There is no introduction here in this email, or information of any kind on the artist, what they sound like, how their music would be a good fit for a radio program, etc.

Do you know what happens to email submissions that look like this?

That's right, they usually get thrown in the trash can. If the emails persist, the sender can be blocked. The vast majority of my radio colleagues operate this way. We have to be selective about what we accept and what messages we read because time is limited for us as well.

"If the ladder is not leaning against the right wall, every step we take just gets us to the wrong place faster." -Stephen Covey, best-selling author of 7 Habits Of Highly Effective People

Most music programs and stations who carry emerging, indie, DIY or unsigned bands and who have any credibility have some form of process that a submission has to go by for their music to be heard. A blanket email sent to 50 or more addresses with no information except a band name and a (lame) intro in the subject line benefits no one, especially you, the artist.

If you seek out a radio promoter, get them to show you a sample of what their messaging looks like before you commit. Also, check on what level of connection they have with their contact list. That fact by itself will be very telling to how connected they are to the stations they have on their list and what their influence is with these contacts.

If a radio promoter says that contacting individual stations or programs "takes too much time," run in the opposite direction. Everything you do in life (and business) involves relationships and communication. It also

involves time.
This reply is very telling of the end goals and methods that a promoter has, and the disservice that can be done to artists.

"The key that underlies it all, to building a rapport and finding that connection, is simple: you have to be able to make people feel good. It's called 'the reward theory of attraction'; simply put, we like people who make us feel gratified and rewarded when we're around them." Harris O'Malley/Doctor Nerdlove, artist and writer

The people who do radio promotion best take the time to do a few things that are essential to you in your station marketing. First, they realize that relationship building takes time and detail. By detail, I'm referring to the practice of crafting specific messages for specific people. That's not a blanket method of writing one thing that you send out to a ton of people on your contact list all at the same time.

Yes, you can write a generic message that covers who you are and what you are trying to do. You can use that base message to send to your whole list. But go back and add a few details pertinent to the recipient to show that you are interested in being a benefit to their product, which is why you're contacting them. Trust me, those specific details go a long way.

People who do promotion right are invested in growing their networks. This is something you as an artist should also take the time to do. Network-growing requires relationship cultivation, which takes time (remember one of the first costs addressed). The folks I highly recommend (see the Appendix at the end of this book for those individuals and companies) for radio marketing and promotion spend time cultivating communication and relationships with their contact base. I know because I'm an example of their work.

What you are offering a radio station is not just your music.

Think about that for a moment and let it sink in.

Stations don't need more music from someone that they've never seen, met or heard of before. More music is everywhere, in greater quantity than any of us can comprehend, understand, or process. The sheer volume (no pun intended) of new music created daily and played on the radio is exponentially greater than it was even a decade ago. Stations and programs aren't looking for more music. They are looking for the right music, great music, that gives their audience something new to enjoy.

Stations create programming for their audiences. They know exactly what their audience enjoys and what it doesn't.

Stations who program for specific groups of people are very synced to their listener base (they have Super Fans too who contribute financially to the operation of the station) and have a commitment to giving that audience something it will value.

What you are offering a radio platform is fantastic music that their audience is wanting more of. All they have to do is hear one of your songs, and they'll be hooked because you provide the sound, storytelling, vibe, and groove that they are hungry for. The offering you are making is for your work to be featured as a part of the great programming that the station is already doing.

"You can make more friends in two months by becoming interested in other people than you can in two years by trying to get other people interested in you." Dale Carnegie, best-selling author of How To Win Friends And Influence People

This piece of inclusion, as well as recognition of the great things the station (or radio/media platform) is currently doing, is a big deal. It's very uncommon for an artist to recognize a platform when they're trying to get station airplay. Since that method of communication is so uncommon, it connects with people very powerfully. I've experienced this first hand when contacting radio stations to get my radio program syndicated in the early days. I made my contact messaging about how our program would benefit the station by adding a new dynamic to the great work the station was already doing. You know what the response was? Overwhelmingly positive.

Does this mean that by taking the time to write a message to each contact that addresses them by name, states their call letters (i.e. KGBT) or website platform, and says 1 good thing about their station resulted in a (positive) response from everyone I contacted? No. That's what happens in a perfect or ideal world, which we do not live in. But I was able to make connections with great people who might have otherwise ignored me and trashed my message.

One key to understand is this: This is a starting point for an ongoing relationship you hope to have with these channels.

Even if you get a response that the station isn't interested, you've created a connection and a dialogue that you can build on. Response is very important, even if it's not the response you want.

"I've come to believe that each of us has a personal calling that's as unique as a fingerprint - and that the best way to succeed is to discover what you love and then find a way to offer it to others in the form of service, working hard, and also allowing the energy of the universe to lead you. "— Oprah Winfrey, media icon and entrepreneur

This is why I encourage those starting this process to take things in increments or steps and don't try and tackle all of this at once.

There is a process to how you go about researching, writing, contacting, and following up that will bring you the results you're looking for through radio play on stations who are wanting your music but don't know where you are or that you exist right now. Soon, you'll solve that problem for them.

You can include some mention of your music in the initial message, but the first contact you make will not be to pitch your music. As we proceed with this process, you'll learn that making the ask is not the first step in building a connection or growing your network. First, you must show yourself to be an uncommon person worth taking an interest in.

Make sure you're ready to move on

1. Name the 4 ingredients to radio promotion.

A).

B).

C).

D).

2. How has radio's role in the promotion of music and entertainment changed in the last decade?

3. What is it that you are really offering a station when you ask for airplay on the radio?

4. Name 1 problem with the sample message presented for music submission.

5. Name 2 things that will really help to make a strong connection with a station manager.
A).

B).

Chapter 5: The Process Of Getting Radio Airplay

"If you do the work, you get rewarded. There are no shortcuts in life." — Michael Jordan, *athlete; NBA legend*

Earlier in this handbook, I said that everything you do as an artist involves a degree of process. The process has been a part of your life in music for quite some time. When you first picked an instrument to play, choosing the right one took time, effort, and consideration.

Later came the process of learning the basics of playing, reading music (or chords of some kind), progressing to more advanced performance and playing techniques, basic songwriting, etc. Everything you do has been a process and will continue to be so until your days are through.

The Radio Airplay Process Includes These Steps

1. Charting Your First 50 Stations To Contact
2. Doing Research
    a. Discovering submission process
    b. Listener type and reach
    c. Format For Chosen Stations
    d. Contact Info on all decision makers
3. Crafting Your Initial Message
4. Follow-up

There is a specific amount of stations listed for a reason. Too often artists try to bite off more than they can handle at one time, mostly because the big picture for many artists is getting your music out to everyone you can. However, take this process in stages, and learn what works best for you.

You don't have to contact 50 radio outlets at one time. If you break down the amount of stations you're going to target in volumes of 25-50, you'll be more focused on choosing the best stations that match your style, your desired audience, and give you the best opportunity to build connections with people.

If 50 seems too big, scale back to 25 or 30. From my experience contacting stations to get The Appetizer Radio Show syndicated, taking this process in doses of 50 stations at a time was the most effective route. When I finished the whole process with the first station group, I could move on to building a new group. This same structure is outlined here.

Section 1: Charting 50 Stations

As an unsigned, DIY, or indie artist (even if you're on a label), your main work involves growing your network and contact base so that your future music releases have a foundation that can be built upon. This growth process requires nurturing existing relationships while creating new ones. Your research will help provide a great platform for that.

First though is charting which stations you're going to target. In some ways, you can tie the first two pieces of this process together. It's optimal to begin with a manageable number to contact for stations and individuals because of all the work that is involved. If you have access to a station list for indie radio, you're still going to need to section off a portion of those stations in your messaging efforts. Don't try to reach everyone at the same time. Also, avoid lumping different types of stations together in one pool, because the follow-up will be that much more difficult.

"Good writing does not succeed or fail on the strength of its ability to persuade. It succeeds or fails on the strength of its ability to engage you, to make you think, to give you a glimpse into someone else's head."— Malcolm Gladwell, author of the best-selling book What the Dog Saw and Other Adventures

Since you have identified the top 3 genres of music you best fit with, pick stations whose programming covers those genres. Begin with stations in your state and surrounding states. It won't serve you as well if you market yourself to Utah radio stations but you live in Georgia. The reason for this is that radio promotion is best utilized when you can tie it to a tour schedule or booking schedule of some kind.

If your band is playing in Georgia, chances are you want to do some Atlanta venues because that's the largest market in the state.

Large markets create an opportunity to get in front of more potential fans of your music.

Plus, larger markets already have more established music cultures and music scenes which are diverse and growing. If you live in Marietta (northwest of Atlanta), you have several areas where you can perform that stations based in the Atlanta area will have carriage.

When a listener hears your song and it really syncs with them, they will look you up online and check to see if you're on streaming services like Pandora or Spotify. After seeing if you have music for sale (or where else they can hear you) they will check your tour schedule, in hopes that you're playing in their area. By starting your radio promotion in regional areas or states nearby, you create a stronger opportunity to connect with people who will follow you and come out to your shows.

"Songwriters write songs, but they really belong to the listener." — Jimmy Buffett, songwriter and author of A Pirate Looks at Fifty

There is a caveat to this method that I'm going to address, and something that can seem to counter the methodology just described. But following this alternative means of radio promotion will require a considerable amount of more time, energy, and money in the long run.

That method is this:

One key benefit of radio airplay is to build your email and social media contact network to solicit for small venues, house shows across the country, and position yourself better to gain a strong team of promotion experts like management and PR agents.

By growing a solid group of contacts, you position yourself better to have a pool of resources to build you up along the way.
New fans may contact you and request a house show or ask you to play at their party. They may offer to pay you to perform. You're going to have to figure out how to get up to Utah, and (hopefully) have a series of shows you can book to pay your route up there.

This method of networking growth has worked for several indie and unsigned artists as they grew their fan base. DIY artists benefit from using house shows and small venues as a means of funding their work. However, it is worth noting that some artists who are using this method and doing so successfully have been doing so for quite a while, and have established their practices and grown their contact list to make the work feasible.

Radio promoters who do great work tie touring and radio promotion together. Radio promotion is one of the best ways to promote a tour schedule, even if that is a house show tour. Syncing your touring with radio airplay gives you the opportunity to do events on-air with radio.

Again, this is usually the product of years of relationship nurturing and cultivations, not an overnight opportunity for those just starting out. But, as you can see, is certainly an opportunity that arises when you commit yourself to improving your process.

Back to the process of radio promotion: pick 50 stations at first. Don't worry about the size of the station or their coverage map (how widespread their radio signal goes). On the front end, you're looking for radio carriage. The amount of stations who play your music isn't as important as having a good base of contacts to begin with. After all, many radio professionals network with each other regularly and share their opinions on the great new music they're playing, which ends up serving as marketing for you.

Once you know the first 50 stations you want to contact because they fit the type of music you do with their programming, you can begin researching them. One of the best resources I've used as a starting place for this process is http://radio-locator.com/. You can search online stations here too. Another great source for credible stations, programs, promoters, and venues is the Indie Bible. Their lists do come with a price tag, but the stations, programs, and professionals listed here are credible and eager to help artists who seek their assistance.

Researching stations can take a little time if you don't know what it is you're looking for.

I'll save you time by telling you exactly what is important
for you to know in researching station contacts:
1. The station frequency number and call letters
(i.e. 89.7 WLNZ)
2. The city the station is located and where their
coverage is *I said size of station and coverage
isn't important but you'll need this little nugget of
info in your first message
3. The format of programming-Do they carry
 independently produced shows, syndicated
programs, have on-air music hosts, etc
4. Station manager names, titles, email, and other
contact info
5. Mailing address

Most of this information should be on 1 or 2 pages
of the station website. Their programming schedule
will show you the format of programs, which can also
provide a good list of secondary outlets to contact
for airplay, especially if you notice some of the same
programs carried on stations from your list. The station
call letters are important because you'll use that info
in your messaging, which shows that you want to offer
something to their specific station instead of just a
blanket message intended for whoever will listen.

You're going to craft a message that speaks to an
individual and shows that you want to be a part of what
that individual is building (or that particular station is
building within their community). This type of messaging
will make you stand out.

"Names are the sweetest and most important sound in any language." Dale Carnegie, best-selling author of How To Win Friends And Influence People

The About Us link on most sites will have a brief history of the station which might include the areas where their signal is broadcast. If they are a web station, or the web extension of an FM station, the About Us might indicate what areas of the state, country, or world that the majority of their listenership resides.

This link should also provide the management contact information. You need names, job titles, email and phone numbers. I suggest creating a spreadsheet with this information for record keeping and reference points, especially as we get into the contacting portion and follow up. You'll want to chronicle who you are getting a response from and what the response is so you don't accidentally contact the same people multiple times.

If you're contacting multiple people at the same station, address each one by their own name. When you receive an email from an unknown address, and it reads: "Attn Media User" or "Dear Customer," how valued does that make you feel? We usually ignore or delete messages sent to us that don't address us by name. Instead, you'll contact people by their name and build instant rapport.

"How you treat the one reveals how you regard the many, because everyone is ultimately a one." Stephen Covey, best-selling author of The 7 Habits of Highly Effective People

The job titles you're looking for are Music Director, Program Manager (or Director), and Station Manager or General Manager. Most indie and public radio stations will have either 1 GM and a program manager or a station manager and a music staff for on-air work. Larger stations will have more staff.

You want to be able to contact as many of these individuals as necessary even if only one of them is responsible for making the decision on music submissions. If you send a message to the wrong person, it is likely they'll respond and tell you who to contact.

If you don't hear back from the person you were supposed to reach, you already have a reply from one staff member and can follow up that way.

Phone numbers can be important in a few ways. One, we're primarily going to address how to contact stations through email methods or the submission forms built into the station sites. Those operate through email submission in some form or capacity. Phone numbers come into play if you want to try to make a more personal connection, but be very careful about how you go about doing this.

Regarding phone numbers, make sure you're getting the main line to the station or program and an extension to the contact you want to reach. It could be hard to tell if the number is a landline or not, so don't worry about that. The phone is not the only method of followup, but is a way to make contact with stations if used properly and professionally.

Some stations get backlogged on the submissions they receive, and it legitimately can take a while for them to have the time to listen and choose yay or nay on your music. Others simply get sidetracked and forget to respond.

PAY ATTENTION TO THE STATION WEBSITE REGARDING PHONE CALLS

I don't like using all caps, but I really want to drive this point home. Some stations and programs are very specific about artists contacting them, including asking artists who submit music not to call and ask questions about their submission. Before you call (or before you decide to call) make sure there's no copy on the station site that says they prefer no phone calls. I have seen stations and programs who are adamantly against that.

If you choose to call a station, remember that your purpose is to build a connection, not demand airplay.

There are some artists who jump to the conclusion that a submission equals automatic airplay. That's never true in radio. By being respectful, humble and thankful, you can do so much to build a connection with the people you contact.

Other contact information can include the station's Twitter handle or Facebook page, or other online methods of communication. The purpose of gaining these contact methods is to do follow up after your submission and to find other ways of reaching out to them. Most stations provide an email address to contact, but not all of them use email in the same capacities. You may discover that one station is very responsive to their Twitter feed but take several days responding to email. Your main goal is to establish a connection and dialogue, so use what works in making that connection.

The mailing address is important because you are doing something that is even MORE uncommon than the other things mentioned here.

Send a Thank-You Note to the stations who respond to you, whether they add you or not. Here's why: The only physical mail that radio professionals receive (and most people for that matter) are either bills or packages with CDs in them, some from contacts and music promoters they know and others from strangers hoping to get their music played.

A Thank-You note is one of the best connection devices on earth because it makes the recipient feel special, valued, and appreciated. When someone does that for you, you can't help but hold them in a higher light than everyone else. You stand to gain a better contact and relationship this way than almost anything else you do.

"I would maintain that thanks are the highest form of thought; and that gratitude is happiness doubled by wonder."— G.K. Chesterton, artist, author, and writer

Speaking of just mailing CDs or music cards (with a download or stream code) as a means of music submission, there are some pros and cons to doing so. The benefits include ease of communication, having all of your info in one place, and savings on postage from not mailing a physical album. The problem with this method can be that you may not hear back from the station if they choose to air or not air your music. Email on the front end at least creates the conversation connection needed to build a relationship starting place.

Section 2: Research

Doing research on radio stations can be a lot of fun because you're not just gathering information, you're having an experience with a music portal that connects with the same people you want to reach with your music. Each station will have a unique set up on their website, their own unique branding, and you can get a pretty good idea of how they connect with their community through their site.

"Research is formalized curiosity. It is poking and prying with a purpose." — <u>Zora Neale Hurston</u>, *American folklorist, and author*

You can also see clearly who their target audience is by spending a little time on their website and listening to their programming. Be sure to listen to the station just a little bit while you're gathering information on the station and its decision-makers. Most FM stations with websites have an online player on their page. Spend a little time listening to the station while you're on the site. This will also give you some potential material for your initial message, such as noting a program host or DJ that you enjoyed listening to. There might be individual hosts or on-air personalities who accept music from indie musicians like you. Their About Us or Our Staff page should have that information.

In your spreadsheet or document (notes), you should have a column/section created for Insights on each station. This is where you'll take a few pieces from the research you're doing and put that info in.
Keep your message brief, but state if the station has a mixed format (meaning more than 2 types of programming are heard such as news, music, talk, classical, etc). If there are several types of music programs, make a note of which ones would be a good fit for your music. If it seems like the station website hasn't been updated in awhile, make a note of that too.

Sometimes in the research process, you will discover stations who present themselves in a way that makes you not want to contact them for any number of reasons. It's good to see for yourself what a station's web presence is and how connected they are with their listener base instead of just blindly messaging contacts without having any reference point. If a web station seems to have an outdated site, this could be an indication of their potential reach or expertise in the field. This is not to say that an older site isn't worth contacting for airplay. Use your best judgement but make note of your findings.

It's very helpful to get 2 contacts per station if you can. This means you'll need 2 rows per station. You want the name, phone number, and email for the Station Manager or General Manager at each station. You'll also need the Program Director's information. If there is a Music Director, get their info. If the station has individual music hosts or DJs and there is contact info for them, add a few but don't overwhelm yourself with that. You can make a point to ask the station management which individual DJ or host would be good for you to contact. Some web stations are run by just one person, so don't let that confuse you.

Section 3: Crafting Your Initial Message

What is the end goal that you are trying to achieve through radio promotion?

This is an important question because the objective reason for using radio airplay to grow your audience is actually larger than just radio itself. At the heart of this process is community building, which is what your initial message is all about. By initial message, I'm referring to the first contact you'll make with the station or program via email.

Remember at the beginning of this handbook when I told you the big mistake I made early on when I was reaching out to radio stations to carry my radio program? My initial message was all about me and my show. I talked only about how the show is a great program for the stations to carry. My intention wasn't entirely selfish because the show is a great way for indie stations to feature music that their audience wants to hear.

However, I didn't frame my initial message with the intention of community building and partnership. The result was little-to-no response from station managers. After a few months of no reply, I had to circle my team back and figure out why we weren't making the traction we wanted. The heart of our endeavor was there, but the way we were reaching out wasn't attractive to the recipients.

This is where everything shifted in my approach.

This shift in approach is what Adam Grant describes in his seminal book Give And Take as **the perspective gap.**

The perspective gap refers to the way we look at situations and circumstances in our lives and careers. If you choose to look at what you're doing from the perspective of the people involved, it drastically changes how you operate, and potentially can lead to much greater success. Grant's description of the difference between the success of George Meyer (who was one of the key writers for The Simpsons and also helped launch the careers of several other great comedy writers) and Jonas Salk (who is credited with inventing the vaccine that cured polio) illustrates very well how seeing things from someone else's perspective is the shift that leads to growth and positive change.

You've probably received some unsolicited emails from companies or marketers that were addressed to "Dear Recipient," or even "To Whom It May Concern." Do you read those emails? I don't, because no one on earth calls me by any of those names. This is another reason why addressing people by their first name is so important. Remember the Dale Carnegie quote earlier. It's true.

Subsequently, when you receive an email or even get tagged by someone on Twitter that is a promotion for someone else's work, with no mention of how you will benefit from it, do you pay attention to those messages? No, I don't either (not much anyways).

This gets to the heart of effective relationship building and networking, which is ultimately the end goal for your radio promotion efforts. When you can get other people to be interested in you before they fall in love with your art or your work, you create a strong bond that will take you so much further than just having a good song that gets a little radio play.

Your initial message should address the strengths and desirable attributes of the station you are wanting to be heard on. You don't need to gush about how much you love everything about the station, and you certainly don't want to lie about having an experience with their programming if you haven't actually had one. Therefore, it's good practice to truly listen to the stations and programs you want to be heard on.

From your notes, add a remark or two in your initial message that sings someone else's praises just a bit. This is a great way to build a friendship or connection right off the bat instead of just pitching your song because it fits their music format.

You want your music heard on the radio so that multiple people in your target audience group has the opportunity to hear your unique sound. However, to get to that point, you have to pass through a few gate-keepers. Station managers are the main ones, and they aren't necessarily always easy to convince, which is why being a community builder is so important to getting them interested in you first, before you present your music.

A station manager or music director has a number of pieces to their daily job. Programming (music selection) is certainly a part of what they do, but there is so much more.

Often times, artists forget that they are contacting people with jobs that include several different assignments and who don't spend all of their time sitting in a room and listening to music. Even music program hosts don't have the luxury of only listening to music to earn a living.

Station managers and program directors receive many (MANY) emails and packages with albums or singles every day, all from artists hoping to get their music heard. This vast amount of submission happens every single day, not every once in awhile.

Imagine for a second that you had strangers contacting you every day and putting something in front of you, wanting you to do something for them without any feedback on the work that you're currently doing, or have done in the past. How would you feel?

Would it seem that the only reason that these people are contacting you is because they want YOU to do something for THEM? And what is the payoff that the station manager gets out of this ordeal? Oh, they get to play that artist's music! Of course, that's all they ever wanted to do.

Please note the sarcasm here, but this is exactly why many artists struggle for months or even years to get their music heard on the airwaves.

How you craft your initial message and how you communicate is the difference maker or deal breaker that can determine whether you're going to get through that gate and into radio airplay. Crafting the initial message is the most important step in this process.

This part listed as the third thing to do, but crafting this message is **the** most important part. You want to build a bridge that links your music to new people. To do that, you have to get certain gatekeepers willing and interested in your work enough to put it on their platform.

You stand to gain so much more by making a strong connection with a gatekeeper who will continue to showcase your music than just give you one spin.

Earlier I mentioned an email that came in recently. I received another email from someone running a small record label. I didn't know they represented a label or where the label was from until I looked him up (Google is a hero in this regard) and found out about their work. Guess what kind of music the label focuses on? Heavy metal and Death metal. Has my radio program ever (in our 12 years of existence) played this style of music? Nope, not once. But, our show is listed on a database of stations that accept music submissions and my email address is available to them to contact. So guess what? I get a random email from a random guy who has no idea who he's reaching out to or if my program is a potential fit for their artists.

As bad as that is for this label and the artists they're

representing, that's not the worst of this issue.
The email to me contained zero (0) information on the band, the song, the album, or anything else. Actually, there was no message.

The subject line said **MP3 attached ATTN: MUSIC DIRECTOR**

 The message had a song name, mention of the vocalist and the label, all printed like a music video caption. There was no message, no intro, no ask, and no reason for me to open the song and discover what the band sounded like.

That email message would have been deleted outright, but I was feeling a little curious. Why would someone who wants their music heard on the radio not at least make an introduction? I responded to the email and simply asked, "How many stations are carrying this song?"

The reply was that they didn't know because they send out that same email to hundreds (if not more) stations and few if any ever reply back. I looked in the recipient portion of my email and saw the laundry list of email addresses this same message had gone out to. I recognized several of the emails and the stations represented. No wonder they're not getting a response. These stations play AAA, indie rock, and some alternative music. Others are mostly News with some Jazz and a little Americana.

Stations program primarily for their audience and make some decisions on what they think sounds best within the parameters of the programming format. This label rep (as well as countless individual artists and some PR companies) didn't bother with finding out who was on this list from a contact standpoint.

That was mistake #1, and also one of the main reasons they weren't getting a response.

I can't say that the other station managers who received that email deleted it right off the bat because they didn't recognize the sender, or if by not having a message they (like me) were not interested in giving something a chance. I also can't say that they didn't open the mp3 file, discover it was a Death Metal song and wonder why it had been sent to them (and then put the email in the trash).

Being selective about who you contact is very important, as well as addressing each recipient by their first name. Think about it this way, if you're in a crowded area and someone you don't know yells out, "Listen to this," are you going to look up and over in that direction or are you going to keep going on your way? Chances are, you're going to keep doing what you were doing and not pay any attention. But if someone says "Hey John, I have something I want to show you," (presuming your name is John) you're going to stop, look up, and give whoever is speaking some kind of attention.

Your initial email message to a station manager is the exact same thing. They don't know you firsthand, not yet, and you are wanting to get their attention so that you can create a connection between their station and your music. The end goal of reaching their audience and converting that audience into your own is what you're working on, so start that connection right. To do that, you need to address them by name, and you need to illustrate that you are unlike every other musician or band out there just trying to be heard. You want to provide something of value to the station and feel some form of gratitude just for having the opportunity to reach out.

"Discomfort brings engagement and change. Discomfort means you're doing something that others were unlikely to do, because they're hiding out in the comfortable zone. When your uncomfortable actions lead to success, the organization rewards you and brings you back for more." -Seth Godin, best-selling author of Are You Indispensable?

By presenting yourself as an Uncommon Person, who is so unique in the way that you do things, the station has a greater reason to listen to your music. Listening is the next logical step that the station takes out of a fascination with wanting to know more about you. Your message is an introduction that should create a bit of an intrigue as well as a relationship spark that creates movement forward for both of you.

Don't say anything that is untrue or over-inflates the positive aspects of your music.

By simply addressing the recipient by name, pointing out that the station (call letters are best to use) provides a great resource for unique programming for the location (city, area or region) and that it would be a wonderful thing to be a part of their programming.

Ask what the music submission process is; don't just attach your mp3 song in the message. The reason is that you want to create a dialogue and correspondence between you and the station. If you can get a manager to respond to your initial request, you have a higher likelihood that they will contact you to tell you when your music is going to be heard on their station. You also have a higher likelihood of getting them to refer you to their contacts. The reply is the connection created.

Include a link to your band website or your Soundcloud or Bandcamp link if that's what you have. You should provide a link to some of your material in the initial message, but be mindful that your real purpose is building the connection. They'll need something to listen to so they can decide if they want to add your music or take that next step. A link to your website, Bandcamp/ReverbNation/Soundcloud (or similar) page or youtube video is an easy solution to do that.

Artists who want radio airplay and are at the point in their musical journey where that is the next step, invest in their presentation by creating a website for the band. Also, it's worth having hard copies of studio recordings to be able to send out to stations or programs that ask for them.

Some stations, music programs, and other media will ask for a hard copy (my program does). Even in a digital world, many respected music programs and stations want a hard copy. Why?

A hard copy (CD) of an album, EP or single represents a musical entity that takes itself seriously and is committed to professional success. Amateurs and garage bands make do with what they can get by with, which is often just free platforms available online. Bands and artists who aren't committed to a professional representation of their art have a much harder time becoming radio-worthy to stations who present a professional offering via their station or program.

The professional representation is similar to a job interview. In some ways, a job interview is exactly what music submission is. Your job as a musician is to create excellent music worth listening to, experiencing and sharing. Through radio, you are offering a service to the station and its audience that provides a quality listening experience.

Should you be given an opportunity to be heard, that exchange of your music played needs to create the positive connection between listener and station. By presenting a professional product and service to the station manager, you're showing up to a job interview with the best look and probability of getting that job.

"Are you ever going to get to the "Crafting Your Message" part of this thing?"

I am. Context can provide such a greater understanding of how everything works when the pieces of the puzzle are explained.

Now that you have new eyes to see what this process looks like, the individuals who make the music selection decisions, and can see a little bit through their eyes and daily lives (from a job task standpoint), you should have a better understanding of the importance of making a strong connection early on.

I'm going to provide you with some example messages, taken almost directly from initial emails I have sent out in an attempt to make connections with station managers, most of whom I had no previous knowledge of or relationship with. The results of messages like this were two-fold:

A). I created a dialogue with station managers that resulted in strong email messaging. Some of the stations (honestly) didn't take on our radio program, but not because they didn't like it. Some didn't have the room on their schedule. Some didn't think that the format fit exactly right, but were still open to the possibility in the future. Others wanted to start airing our radio show right away, which created a different kind of connection.

B). Connection doesn't mean a YES response. Connection means reply and dialogue. I was able to establish a connection with new people that I contacted later and built a strong network with.

There are stations in my network that don't air our radio show, and I'm OK with that. I value the relationship connection so much more because that still benefits me, and I am a benefit to my station contact more than just being a program provider.

I trust and believe that the future holds all kinds of great opportunities for growth and prosperity. Not receiving a YES right now doesn't mean the answer will always be NO. All I need to do is maintain the relationship. You never know when doors will open up down the road with people in your contact list. This is why networking is so valuable.

For some music media platforms (online and FM), there is a bit of a sales process to getting your content aired on their station. That's not to say that you have to become a salesman to get radio play.

DO NOT offer money to get airplay. Some stations and programs do that sort of thing, but it is so unethical and frowned upon by real radio and media when an artist offers money for airplay.

Think about it: If all you had to do was pay a little money to get heard on the radio, what would that say about the quality of the content or even the value of the artist's work? It certainly doesn't speak very highly of a commitment to excellence from the station, let alone any sort of value for what the audience wants and appreciates.

By addressing individuals, asking questions, and talking through the process of getting your music heard, you are "selling yourself" to the station manager on who you are as a person. You are creating that intrigue and connection that you want the manager to have so that he/she will take the next step: listen to your music and add you to their station's programming.

You can't get airplay until your music is heard by the gatekeeper (i.e. the station or program manager). Once your music is heard, then the opportunities present themselves. However, often times music isn't heard or time isn't taken to check out an artist because the musician hasn't given the station rep a reason to care about them beyond just a music offering.

Using A Strong Subject Line

The subject line is a very important part of reaching out to new people, and can be something that confuses artists the first few times. What has worked for me is making a simple subject line that draws the recipient in to want to see what the message is about. Remember, you're contacting station managers and program hosts who provide music for listeners. One easy thing you can put in your subject line is "Music Programming Question" or "Music Programming Request." At the heart of your endeavor, you are going to ask a question.

If you were to put "Indie Artist Seeking Airplay" in the subject line, you might not get the attention you're looking for or create the opportunity for connection. As you'll see in a moment, you're going to illustrate your appreciation for their programming and showcase how you'd like to be a part of it. When you make the station's programming your subject, you create a stronger opportunity for the manager's attention to your message.

The Initial Message

Now for the meat and potatoes. Crafting your message includes 5 elements, 3 of which should be included to make a strong connection. If you can get by with only 1 or 2 of these, let me know. I'll be interested in knowing how you did it. The 5 elements are:

1. Manager/Director's first name
2. Station call letters and location
3. Type of programming the station has that your music fits into
4. Ask about the music submission process
5. Link to hear or download your music or ask how it can be sent by mail

To save yourself time, I have a few templates you can pull from. It's ok to take these templates and insert the appropriate information per station and use it again and again. I also encourage you to take what I have here and make your own modifications to it to fit the way you communicate. You want to be authentic and speak in your natural voice.

You'll also notice the mood or approach that these messages have. You're not throwing your music out there and hoping it will be heard. You're also not demanding airplay (yes, many artists do that and are offended when they are turned down).

You're making a connection and showing that you appreciate the station manager's time, their interest, and the opportunity to be a part of what they are already doing (providing great music programming for their listeners).

Here are 2 examples of an initial email message. Use these examples to **create your own message** instead of copying and pasting information alone. Sincere communication goes a long ways.

1. Dear (Station Manager),

In looking at stations in (state), I found (station call letters) and really like what you all are doing. Independent music is something I've been drawn to for a long time, both as a fan and as a musician.
I enjoy your program format and the unique sounds that (station) showcases.

Seeing that you feature music programming that appeals to real supporters of the arts, I wanted to see if you accept music submissions and what is involved in that process.

Our band is (name) and our style fits perfectly with your

station because we (brief description of music and style). Our EPK is available at (link). I can send you a hard copy of our album or a digital version if that is preferable. Thank you for the opportunity to connect with you. I look forward to hearing back from you and providing great music for your audience.

Thank you, -Signed-

2. Hello (Station Manager),
I enjoy your station and your programming for (city). Public and community radio stations provide such a unique offering on the radio that isn't found elsewhere. Who can I speak with about music submissions for airplay on (station call letters)?

I imagine that you get tons of people sending you music all the time asking for airplay. I'd like to make a connection with you and see how our band can be a resource in providing more great music programming for (station). Our band is [name] and we sound like (brief description of music). You can hear our sound at (website and EPK link). Let me know what your process is for music
submission and what form (digital or hard copy) you prefer. Thank you for this opportunity. I look forward to connecting with you and serving your audience.

-Signed-

What To Send To Stations By Snail Mail:

Whether you're going to mail a station a package with your music or submit everything strictly through the Internet, there are some specific things you need to make sure you send out. They are:

1. The Music (CD or Digital copy). Make sure the recording is at the highest possible quality. Many stations will accept MP3s but make sure the kbps is high (128kps or greater). If you send a low-quality recording, you're throwing your work away.

2. A song list that contains the track names of everything delivered. Include a note on any song that contains profanity, indicate it as FCC-Warning and state the word in the line that's used. If the song contains multiple swear-words, state that. The song list should also have 2 or 3 songs selected that you want the radio station to consider specifically for airplay. You can say "Looking For Adds with (Track Name)" or "Featuring The Single (Track Name)." These tracks are your best songs. Most radio outlets aren't going to listen to your whole album so give them your best work and tell them which songs those are. If you're sending MP3 files, make sure the artist or band info, song track names, album title and artwork for the album is in the Metadata of the files. Most radio stations won't take the time to research your track or album info if it's not already in the files.

3. A One-Sheet EPK or Press Kit. Yes, it's just one sheet because you don't want too much clutter for the radio programmer to have to sort through. Your one-sheet can include a band or artist image, your contact information, where you've been featured (other radio stations or online platforms), and at least one or two reviews of your music. If you don't have any reviews yet, try submitting your music to some sites for paid reviews. Fluence.io is a great outlet for that service (see the Appendix at the end of this book for a list of sites and links to aid you in this process of getting reviews). If you have a standard press kit that is a few pages, edit something down to a single page and send that with your music.

If you have an EPK (electronic press kit), you can send a link to it in the message. I don't advise attaching the EPK to your initial message email because attachments can be a red flag to stations. However, if you are going to do a CD run by way of mailouts (specifically for labels and radio promoters), include the press kit in the mail out.

Don't only send a CD to stations or programs with no material or information on your band, music or contact info. This can be a little bit of a misnomer since you don't have the connection yet but you are sending the hard copies of music out. We receive CDs mailed all the time that are just a disc and no info on the band or contact information. How will the band or artist find out if their music was featured on any of the programming that they spent money on mailing to stations without providing some form of contact information?

Press kits are an essential part of your presentation to not only radio but to other forms of media. If you are at the place where you are truly Radio-Ready, get a press kit made. EPK's allow you to include all the information, reviews, description, images, etc that a traditional press kit has, as well as give you the freedom to email it instead of putting it in the mail. I recommend having a hard copy of your current press kit and modifying its contents on a quarterly or bi-annual basis as you receive more press reviews, airplay, and performances with other artists.

Make sure your press kit contains contact information for you or your band representatives (manager, booking agent, etc). I received a press kit and a great CD from an emerging artist that we ended up doing a feature review on, but his press kit had no contact info on it. It took us a while to go through the process of contacting him to notify him that he had a review. Most media outlets aren't going to go out of their way to contact you, so give them what they need to reach out to you up front.

Should I include my Twitter or Facebook page in my email message?

You can, but your initial message is about making connection. Plus, most bands who only have a Facebook fan page or similar web presence are not yet radio-ready from a branding standpoint. By stating that your music is available only on those sites, you're implying that you expect the radio contact to do all the work and go "discover" your sound.

That works at times, but isn't as effective as making an initial connection.

Section 4: Follow-Up

Remember all those details I said you needed to get when you were making your list and doing research? All the little pieces of information that seemed at the time to not have anything to do with sending an initial email, like phone numbers and mailing address?

These key ingredients are what are going to help make you stand out as an individual and as a person that station managers want to help out, even if the term "helping out" isn't what they would call it.

Before you send your first email, set up a schedule to start this process of emailing and contacting people that can be chronicled with the information of each station that you plan on emailing. By setting up a schedule, you can keep better track of who you've reached out to and what their response was. Create the columns for each of these data points:

-Station Call Letters
-State/Location
-Format
-Notes/Info
-Manager Name/Position1
-Email 1

-Manager Name/Position2
-Email2
-Date Contacted
-Response Date
-Response
-Follow Up Date

Here's a screenshot of what that looks like as an Excel
document (which is what I used)

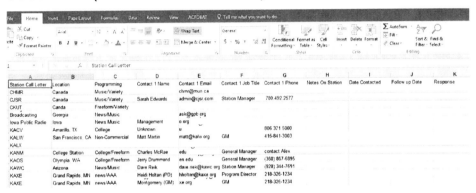

Notice that there are two different fields for 2 separate
managers and their positions and emails. The reason for
this is that many stations and programs have multiple
people in charge of music or programming selection.

Often times a Music Director or Program Director has a
role in selecting music for programming.

The Station Manager or General Manager, however, has
the final say. If you only contact one member, you have a
50-50 shot at creating the connection.

However, when you contact both, there is a chance that the two individuals will talk about receiving a note from you and one having listened or responded. Your followup endeavors increase your potential when you can create a connection with two individuals from one station.

Follow up is an ongoing process that involves you reconnecting with your contact list after a period of time.

You're going to follow up initially 2-3 weeks after sending the first email to check and see if the recipient(s) have had a chance to get your email. Most of the stations who will be interested will reply to you within a few weeks, but sometimes emails slip through the cracks.

The time between your initial email and the follow-up may seem long. There are times when my team and I have so much stuff going on with our programming and other events that we can't get to look at any of the submissions for several days or even a few weeks. It's not a matter of people ignoring you necessarily, as much as there being so much music to sift through for too few people. Stations and programs of any size deal with this constantly, so try to keep that frame of reference.

Your initial follow-up can be through email, social media or the other contact information you gathered.

Phone calls can be made but do so with care. Not everyone treats phone calls from prospective artists the same way.

Important: When NOT To Call: As stated before, there are some stations and music radio outlets that will accept music submissions, but do not want to receive phone calls about submissions. The Radio platform's website should state what their submission criteria is and possibly will say whether they accept calls from artists or not. Pay attention to this and make a note of it on your spreadsheet.

When you get someone on the phone, you have potentially created a personal connection. This call is to reaffirm the process of submission. Take only a couple of minutes talking to the manager and then thank them for their time. If they ask you questions about your music, answer them with specific, but brief statements. Don't tell your life story. At some point, they may interview you and then you'd have the opportunity to share more.

A few other considerations about phone calls are worth considering. The station may not do phone calls to their management from artists. Simply respect that and ask for an alternative form of communication. If they do accept calls, be respectful of their time. Talking too much for too long can be a turn-off to new people who don't know you. Honor their time (as well as your own) and get the response you're looking for which is: how can I get my music in front of you for airplay consideration?

There are other ways of following up aside from email and phone calls. Every person on earth has a different preferred method of communication.

Some folks prefer email over phone calls. Others use their social media channels like Facebook or Twitter as their primary communication tool, especially with people they don't know face to face. You can follow the same style of communication in reaching out to a radio platform by contacting them on Twitter or Facebook to ask a question. Still, it's important to exercise brevity and gratitude in your messaging.

Some stations also have online forms that you can fill out to ask questions or make submissions. Contacting stations through these portals is an effective way to make a connection. If you don't hear back from a station after several weeks (and you filled out a form initially), try following up by email or some other contact form.

If you get a response email that asks you to email them your music or send a CD, simply do what they ask. If they send you to a form online that you fill out for music submissions, do that. Wait a few weeks after you've done what was asked and call the person who replied to you to see if they've had a chance to hear your music. If they have, ask for some feedback or see if the song will be on their station in the near future.

If they haven't listened to your music yet, don't worry. Making the phone call is a great reminder for them to go back and check out your work.

You might ask if there is a point in time in the next week when they will have time to listen and get back to you.

Either way, thank them for their time and consideration.

The last element you were to look up in making this process work best is a mailing address for each station contact. The reason you need this information is not so you can just mail the station a copy of your CD for airplay. If the station asks for a hard copy, send it. You need the mailing address to do the most essential (and again, uncommon) element of follow-up: Send a Thank-You card.

When was the last Thank-You card you received? It could have been following a wedding you attended for a friend, or maybe a note your grandma sent you to say thanks for coming to see her for her birthday. It's pretty out of the ordinary to get a Thank You card anymore, which makes receiving one very special.

I know the power of Thank You notes from artists because it's been true for me, and for several of my colleagues in this industry. I've experienced this with select musicians who have gone on to make very successful careers with their music. After having their song featured (or after being interviewed for a feature on the radio), certain artists have mailed me cards or short letters just saying thank you. These artists include Sandi Thom, Jerzy Jung, William Fitzsimmons, The Lone Bellow and Thriving Ivory.

The impression that those little notes left led to a greater connection because I keyed in on new notifications, messages, and mailings from them in the future.

In short, their little note left such a strong impression that I pay more attention to their future communications. That's the connection you want to create.

"When life is sweet, say thank you and celebrate. And when life is bitter, say thank you and grow."— Shauna Niequist, author of Bittersweet: Thoughts on Change, Grace, and Learning the Hard Way

What does your Thank-You note need to say? Simplicity is the best policy. Don't spend much time gushing about how the radio airplay completely changed your life, or try to write Thoreau-quality prose. Just say thank you for the opportunity to talk and have your music featured on their station. Sign your name and be sure to include your band name or music name (if different than your individual/ personal name).

One added thing that helps build a stronger bond between you and the station or program is to include a little SWAG in your mailing, such as a sticker, pin, or poster autographed by the band. I used to decorate my office at the radio station with SWAG that artists sent me. We like that stuff, and it builds a psychological connection between radio and artist.

Having done all of these elements, you can move on to the next group of station contacts and repeat the process.

Your follow-up will be ongoing, and should involve a series of conversations with different folks over a period of time.

"We get good at what we do." -wisdom from a good friend and mentor Larry Sabin, entrepreneur owner of Comics & Collectibles in Abilene.

If you try contacting a station or music program and do all of these things but get no response, let it go. You're not going to connect with every station you reach out to. I wish it were different, but that's the way it is for all of us. You need to be settled with that. However, once you start getting stations responding to you, the process becomes much easier because you see patterns with how managers operate. You learn new little ways to reach out and build connections. And you gain more credibility and marketability.

Remember when I said that we added 5 stations to our carrier list in the first few years? That seems like such a small number, but it was a big deal for us as a smaller indie program with a tiny staff. You should have better results due to the difference in what you're offering (a few songs to feature instead of a weekly 2-hour program). Regardless, once you get momentum going, don't slow down or stop. It's important to keep your networking active.

Station managers and those who pick music for programs network and talk to each other.

Many times they chat with each other for the purpose of hearing what band or artist someone else has picked up on that they should tune in to or carry. When you make a strong connection with a station by having a great musical story to tell, a strong sound worth experiencing, and you match that with being a personable individual, you have created the best opportunity for your music to be talked about and shared by the decision-makers of radio. Being talked-up by radio programmers is one of the best marketing vehicles on earth, and it is also one that you can't buy, making it even more valuable.

Do you also remember at the start of this book when I said that changing your mindset on how you operate and making 1-1 connections with people is like Growth Hacking the radio and music industry? Now you know the How-To that makes this work. Contacting individuals and building relationships and connections with them is uncommon, and not what 99% of artists or marketers do to grow their platforms. Since most people are essentially spamming their way to gain an audience, when you do the uncommon thing, you make a much stronger impression which leads to a greater potential for reciprocal connection.

<u>Make sure you're ready to move on</u>

1. List the 4 steps involved in the radio airplay process.

A).
B).
C).
D).

2. What might cause a station manager to delete your email immediately without opening it or checking out your music?

3. Name 2 uncommon things I've suggested you do to make yourself really stand out to station managers from this process.

A).
B).

4. What is the real purpose of your initial message to a station manager or music program host?

5. What 3 things do you send to radio stations to showcase your music?
A).
B).
C).

6. Name 3 of the 5 things you need to include in your initial message.

A).
B).
C).

7. Why is follow-up so important?

Chapter 6: Using Radio To Your Advantage In Audience Building

Many musicians stop their own progress by making one part of the process their end goal. What I mean by this is that they believe that getting radio airplay, or even landing a licensing deal, is the final result to achieve the success they want. Striving for just radio airplay as the single target is going to result in you not achieving the *real* end result you should be aiming for: sustainable audience connection.

As I stated earlier, you make music for yourself and for a specific group of people who connect with your unique offering. This is your ideal target audience, also known as your core fan base. Your target audience is a smaller group of people than the collective number of folks who will follow you at some point in their lives. Your collective fanbase consists of people who have given you different levels of attention, dedication, and financial support. Your goal with radio airplay is to be able to reach more people who potentially are your collective fanbase, as well as sync with individuals who fit your core audience profile.

Do you know the type of person who best associates themselves with your music or story? These people constitute your core audience (and are also referred to as your Super-Fans in my other books and materials).

They come from different parts of the country and all around the world. They are different ages, genders, and work in different industries. But there are some specific things about them that are very similar. Your ability to recognize the commonalities in your fan base gives you a dynamic insight into how to grow a sustainable audience connection.

Your core audience are the people who will keep your music career going even if you never have a commercially hit song, or don't reach a music licensing deal on TV or film. What if you don't reach platinum record sales? That's never been a prerequisite for music success. Your core audience also can keep your music wheels going even if you never perform in an amphitheatre in front of 50,000 people. All of these achievements are what most musicians want to experience in their musical journey, because reaching these points usually indicates levels of great success. However, you can reach all of these plateaus and still not be able to pay your bills or grow your musical brand.

A sustainable audience connection keeps you front and center with the right people who are most drawn to your music. Every time they hear your song on the radio or see something posted about you online, it re-ignites the fire they have for your sound and storytelling. When you post a request or sign-up for hosting house shows across the country, these people respond in droves. When you announce your new album release, they get the pre-purchase version.

If you release a special EP with new songs and a few covers, they snatch it up right away. Your tour schedule becomes a part of their calendar. All of these elements keep finances coming into your music coffers which keep your career going.

A few examples of this dynamic are illustrated in the music careers of Josh Garrels, whose fan base consists of over 200,000 people subscribed to his email list. Every time he releases something new, his audience responds in droves because he has made such a strong connection with them specifically.

Another great example is Brandi Carlile. Spend any amount of time on her Facebook Group (the group is Brandi Carlile Oh How I Love Thee) and you'll see the dynamic effects she has on her super fans, who consistently grab every song, album, special merchandise, and attend her shows.

Radio fits into this super fan growth because the more target stations you have playing your music, the more target ideal fans you are getting in front of. Use radio to grow your core audience (super-fan) base so that you can build the connection with them that they are seeking by enjoying and buying your music.

In business and marketing, there is a principle of impressions-to-sales-conversion that describes the amount of times someone has to experience something before they spend money on it.

Depending on the industry, product or service the number of impressions may be many before someone is willing to spend money on it.

With music, where many listeners and fans expect to get what they want for free, you're going to have to connect with a different type of music fan to create a conversion opportunity.

There still are plenty of music fans and supporters who believe in supporting the artists they enjoy with their money, be it by going to live shows or buying music (digital, CD, vinyl, etc). However, these types of fans are not as common as the everyday John Doe, who just wants to listen or stream a song and never own anything associated with the artist. You will attract several John and Jane Does in your music career. Don't sweat them. Targeted radio airplay puts you in front of people who think about your art different, and support it.

This is another reason I'm very much against artists paying for radio play. Audiences who tune into radio or web outlets where the criteria is not set specifically for quality and listening experience (and allow people to buy the opportunity to be played) are creating audio content for people who just want a handout and not support what they hear.

Doing research on stations gives you that insight into knowing the quality of media outlet you are going to solicit to and be a part of.

As an artist of sound and songwriting quality, you want to be associated with stations who value quality connections. Doing so is in your best interest with audience connection, as well as ongoing endeavors with stations.

Would you like to get an interview on the radio, or do an in-studio session with a station? Your follow-up endeavors from the initial contact provide the groundwork for that to happen. When you get a response from a station manager, you've opened a doorway for potential further engagement with that station.

At some point (preferably after they commit to playing your music) you can ask about the criteria for doing an interview on-air. Don't demand an interview, or assume that because they played your song that they owe you an interview. Yes, artists have exhibited this attitude towards our show and several of my colleagues regarding interviews and radio features. It can be a bridge-burner, and it is something to avoid. There is a chance that the station or music program will reach out to you to initiate the interview or feature process. You don't have to wait for them to reach out, but you do need to be respectful of them and their decision-making process.

The stations you reach out to are targeted for reasons beyond just audience specifics. You should be able to gauge (based on location and proximity to your area) whether or not you could feasibly tour that part of the country. Do your best to associate radio airplay with your tour schedule or house show booking.

If you live in Chicago and want to do a 5 state tour through Illinois, Indiana, Michigan, Ohio and Pennsylvania, make a point to get some radio airplay in the regions and areas of those states where you want to play. If you haven't made a tour schedule before you do a radio push, don't worry.

The stations who pick up your music can help provide a roadmap of areas where you can tour through.

Why should touring and radio go together? Airplay alone might not give you the return on your music investment that you are seeking. This is one reason why it's missing the target to just make radio airplay your end goal.

When radio can work along with a touring band, you have more opportunities to get in front of people. Getting in front of people creates the impression necessary to convert listeners into fans through monetary exchange. The experience you provide through your music in just the audio/radio form can be enough to get someone to purchase a single and eventually an album. When you can perform that song live, and create a powerful experience for someone to have, they will be more likely to buy your album, grab your merchandise, and also share that experience with their friends online and in person. This experience is what leads to further opportunities for you with new fans.

I've worked with several artists who use radio along with a national tour to promote their latest album release.

When done right, the album sells well because people who are listening to particular radio stations are the types of music fans most prone to buying music and attending live performances. Other artists have used the radio airplay they've received over the years to create strong tour schedules that involve specifically house shows and small venues for more intimate engagement.

The mantra for house shows is that if you can get 15-40 people to attend and be paid for the attendance (either through a cover fee or a donation), and set a specific number of dates, you can have a profitable music career that doesn't involve having to sign to a label or be forced to play venues that aren't suited for your style. Radio airplay gives you a key opportunity in making those live venues successful.

If you target international stations, touring might not be as readily available to you from the outset, but is certainly achievable. I know several artists who have had international radio play and were able to tour the world playing small venues and house shows, marketing their sound using radio airplay to draw in fans to shows. Artists like Kelley McRae, Susan Enan, Flatfoot 56 and others have done this for years.

<u>Make sure you're ready to move on.</u>

1. Is radio airplay or music licensing the end goal for your music? Why or why not?

2. What should you pair with your radio airplay to get the maximum results for your efforts?

3. What should you never offer a radio station to get airplay? Why?

4. Describe how you can use radio to build and grow your core audience base.

Chapter 7: Radio Partnered With Your Social Media Platforms

It's true that radio and entertainment as a whole are playing a numbers game. It's tempting to confuse the numbers that don't matter with those that do. This is one reason why I strongly urge artists, musicians, entrepreneurs, and small businesses to avoid doing what countless people have attempted: buying followers on social media.

Radio stations and programs might look at your following on your Facebook or Twitter page to see how established you are. More than likely, they want to see that you have a social media platform, that you're using it to connect with your fans, and that there are actual people following you and not a ton of bots or fake accounts.

It is not a prerequisite for you to have a monumental following on your social channels for you to be considered for radio airplay or feature on radio websites. However, there are many musicians out there who try to play the numbers game by giving a false impression of how great their fan base actually is. You see it when there's an artist with a substantial following on Twitter, but their sound leaves little to be desired. If you took the time to look at their followers, you'd find several bots or fake users. How does a fake Twitter account who is following you help you?

You can buy followers, but you can't truly buy connection, least of all you can't buy real friends. Facebook changed the way we see connection when they launched their Like platform and follow. You can "Add A Friend" with someone you don't know at all, simply based on the click of a mouse. Anyone can Like any professional page without having an experience with the person, their product, service, offering, etc. Twitter is the same. Other social media outlets provide a platform to initiate connection without having to have a face-to-face encounter.

"You can make more friends in two months by becoming interested in other people than you can in two years by trying to get other people interested in you."— Dale Carnegie, best-selling author of How to Win Friends and Influence People

This is not to say that having and building a following on social media is wrong, or that it doesn't play a role in your audience growth, particularly with radio. It does play a factor and has a role. However, keep your focus on building solid connections with the real people who experience your music instead of trying to give an impression that isn't authentic regarding your true fan base. It's much better for your music success and growth to be firmly connected with 500 core audience fans who regularly attend your gigs, buy your music, and spread the word about your releases than to spend money trying to give the impression that you're more successful than you really are.

I'm referring to buying followers, not necessarily advertising on social media. That's a different subject altogether.

There's a big difference between the amount of followers you have and the influence your work creates. You might be able to buy followers, but you can't buy influence. Your underlying mission through radio promotion is the same as your social media platforms: community building. Community building is about cultivating a connection with what matters to other people.

"We can't be afraid of change. You may feel very secure in the pond that you are in, but if you never venture out of it, you will never know that there is such a thing as an ocean, a sea. Holding onto something that is good for you now, may be the very reason why you don't have something better." — C. JoyBell C., author, poet, philosopher

As a musician, you are a storyteller with an amazing opportunity to impact people's lives in a profound and emotional way. Your tales, songs, melodies, beats, and talents can be used to do so much more than simply entertain. By connecting with radio stations who are making a difference in the communities they serve, your music matches the mission they have set forth to achieve, which is how you provide great value to their programming.

Marketing experts have shown that the best ways to grow your connection with your following on social media is to operate the 80/20 rule, which means that 80% of your content is connection with your community, sharing other's posts, asking questions, and facilitating conversations. The other 20% is self-promotion. More often, however, we see musicians operating the other way around. Are most of your social media status updates and posts simply promoting your next show, you new release, or begging your fans to buy your music? If so, re-evaluate the 80/20 rule and see how you can use social media to connect with what truly matters to your audience.

Make sure you're ready to move on.

1. What are 2 reasons why you don't have to have a million Twitter followers to get radio airplay?

2. You can buy followers but you can't buy _____.

3. What relationship does your social media platforms have with your radio promotion?
How does your music match the mission that radio stations have?

4. How does the 80/20 rule apply to you in marketing your music?

Chapter 8: Budgeting For Music Promotion (Appendix 1)

At the very beginning, I told you that doing radio promotion yourself would cost you your time, patience, and a little money. How much money did I mean?

I've worked with artists who spend large amounts of money on their promotions and marketing, but are wary about spending any to promote their music through radio. I have a hard time understanding this. Radio promotion is one of the best ways to be heard by music fans, especially those seeking to experience something off of the beaten path of the pop music realm. But to get your music out to radio stations, you need to be willing to spend a little money.

I am NOT talking about paying stations to play your music. That method of radio promotion was fairly prominent in the 1970s where artists would pay DJs a few bucks on the side to get their record on the air. It became known as Payola and was illegal for many years. It's a bit of a gray area now on whether payola is a legal way to get your music heard. Either way, it is certainly unethical. I advise you to run away from folks who offer to play your music on the radio for a fee or a rate. It's not a practice to take on.

However, you will have to spend some money getting your music into the hands of radio professionals, mostly by way of the mailman. Mailing a CD can cost anywhere from $1.50 to $5.00 depending on the size of the package and the distance traveled.

This is one reason why many artists only want to do digital submissions because it removes the cost element of paying for postage. However, this is one reason it's so important to make connections with the radio outlets you're wanting to be heard on. Once you establish a connection and a station or program asks you to mail a disc to them, there's a very high likelihood that your CD will be listened to in its entirety or at least sampled for a longer period than just a music stream online.

You will need to determine what your promotion budget is and stick with it. You should include this element of your expenses with your marketing budget and have a portion of money set aside just for postage to stations.

Another element of radio promotion that could have a price tag is what you set up on your own website to host your songs or EPK. Depending on the size of your audio files, images, and other materials in your EPK, you may need to increase your bandwidth option on your website. If you're only using Bandcamp or Reverbnation as your online platform for your music, this is something else to look into when you start promoting for radio.

Most reputable stations and programs want to feature music from artists who have invested in their own web platform instead of operating from a URL extension to Soundcloud (or similar). Those options are free, but they don't work to your benefit in a branding standpoint or from a position of professionalism like your own website does.

While submitting music to online outlets such as blogs is not the same as radio, many radio platforms have a blog associated with their offering, usually as part of their website. I do that with The Appetizer Radio Show as a way to give our fans more opportunities to connect with emerging music aside from the weekly radio show. There are several other stations, programs, and outlets who do the same.

Since indie music sites are bombarded with requests for features, and often our inboxes are full of submissions, many sites will offer a fee-based review. This can be a great way to make a solid connection with a media platform which can benefit you in the long run. Featured reviews, even those that may cost a few bucks, provide great content for you to use in your press kit to market to new stations. It also puts your music in front of a more focused audience group.

Why should I pay for someone to review my music? What can't they just do it for free? They are reviewing music on their site anyways. I'm simply giving them free content. Shouldn't that be payment enough?

This is the line of thinking that gets too many musicians off course. First off, there is not a drought on good music in the world, so submitting music to a media outlet, be it a blog or a radio platform, for free in the name of content alone is not a fair trade. Too many artists (the 99%; the common artist) will throw their music at someone and expect them to listen. There are too many artists to listen to in this way.

However, when an artist is willing to part with a few dollars for a thorough review on someone else's platform, some very important things can take place. First, you are guaranteed to be listened to and have attention paid to your music. Most review sites are looking for great music to showcase and don't want to spend their time bashing someone else's work. Second, the impetus on your music being Radio-Ready comes into play when a feature will cost you something. You'll do more work to get your sound in the best place possible, as well as make sure your songwriting is Top-Shelf when you have a little skin in the game too. Lastly, a different kind of connection is made when money changes hands. There's a bond that takes place that creates an opportunity for the blogger or site to provide more of a window to their audience base on your behalf because you're paying for their time, expertise, and attention. That little detail can go a long way.

Keep all of this in a frame of reference for your overall budget, but don't be surprised if you come across online outlets who put a fee with their reviews.

The reason for this is that they want to spend their time reviewing great music, and most artists who are willing to put some skin in the game (their money) have higher quality music than those who just want a handout. Take the time to research the platforms you want to be featured on who have a paid review as an option before you spend any money on the endeavor.

Some other options for submission that can come with a price tag include two services that I use for both The Appetizer Radio Show and for the work I do as a music coach. They are MusicSubmit.com and Fluence.io. Music Submit is a resource specifically for submission to radio outlets in specific formats. Fluence.io is a submission for feedback, critique, and potential social media shares. It's also a great way to get your music in front of radio hosts, station managers, and other music influencers and curators. Both services come with a fee for submission. Factor this option into your music budget for future opportunities for growth.

Recommended Radio Promoters

At the start of this book, I told you that my experience working as a music program host and music curator has put me in contact with some radio promotions professionals who do great work. I can speak for their excellence because when I get submissions from them, 9 times out of 10 the artists are well-produced, the press kit material is top-shelf, and my radio team is very pleased with the music.

It's not a guarantee that everything these folks send in will get airplay on our show, but I do get excited when I check the mailbox and have something from them because it's usually very good music.

However, their excellent marketing and station/program promotion comes at a price, which is why budgeting for radio promotion is so key. You can get your music added to hundreds of stations on your own without spending a ton of money using the guidelines I've laid out here. The professionals who excel at radio promotion do put a fee on their service, and I believe if your music is at the radio-ready point, it can be well worth the fee.

Some of the radio promotions professionals I've worked with over the years include Right Arm Resource, JB Brenner, Missing Piece Group, True Tone Group, Razor & Tie, N3w Level Management, and Dangerbird Promotion. There are several others. Do your research and find out what works best for you.

Make sure you're ready to go on

1. Why should you budget for marketing and promotions with the radio if payola is not what you're going to do?

2. How do you see yourself as a music entrepreneur, having seen the process of radio promotion and marketing for musicians?

3. What are 2 reasons to send a radio station a CD? What are 2 reasons not to?

4. What role does your EPK serve in the promotion and marketing of your music?

5. With everything that is involved in the radio promotion process, would you rather do all of this yourself or pay someone else to do it? (If your answer depends on how expensive it is, the really good companies can be quite expensive, fyi)

Chapter 9: Supplemental Hints & Tips (Appendix 2)

Who to send a CD to and who to send a digital recording to:

Some radio stations and programs will only accept digital files of music and will not accept hard copies or CDs. Other programs only accept CDs and frown on receiving digital copies. I've fallen into both sides of this, only accepting CDs until very recently. Let me illustrate to you a few reasons why some stations prefer one way or the other, and what this should mean to your planning for contacting stations.

Stations/Programs Who Only Accept Digital Music:
Some outlets have too many CDs and would prefer just having a digital copy that can be listened to from their computer and then sent to a program host or to their automation system for airplay. This process can seem a little less involved than having to get a CD into someone else's hands and then creating the track upload. Digital copies are a little easier to deal with from a receiving standpoint, and can be easier to manage. It's understandable why a station or program would want to downsize the potential clutter that infinite CD submissions could cause.

Digital only submissions allows a station rep to listen directly from their computer and make a decision on the spot without having to fiddle with CDs and players. However, due to the music being in digital only form, it can lead to messages or submissions being deleted with no reply back to the sender on the submission results. That's if you send a straight MP3 file copy with your submission.

Stations/Programs Who Only Accept CDs:
I've done submissions by CD only for several years and in many ways, it's been a great way to accept music from unsolicited senders, most of whom had no previous relationship with the program or myself. Here's why we (until very recently) only accepted submissions by way of CD: it keeps our email from backing up with tons and tons of poorly constructed submissions, attached files, and serves as a great filter for musicians of quality.

Too many artists only have digital copies of their music. I firmly believe that is a problem for the artist, and potentially can keep them from growing their fan base and (most importantly) being able to financially profit from their music. When an artist takes the step towards CD distribution, it's a fairly significant financial investment. To do so, you're illustrating that you take your music seriously and want it to grow. You're not just throwing a recording out there and thinking people will like it just because you do.

The other big reason I prefered the CD only submission is because some of the biggest players in music radio operate that way.

NPR Music does not accept digital submissions, which is one of the main reasons we went in this direction. They do accept music submissions, but you have to do it by mail and CD. The reasoning for them is similar to ours.

How To Know Which To Send:

In your initial email to station management, you've asked what the process is for music submissions. Not every station rep you contact will necessarily reply, which is why the follow-up phone call is so important. Once you have an idea of which they prefer (digital or CD copy), you're in a good position because you've already made contact with the station rep. When they receive your music, they should remember the connection established.

You greatly improve your chances of the manager or rep remembering you if you include a note or short letter in your CD package (mail) just saying hello and thanking them for their time talking with you. Little things like that can go a long way.

How To Tell If Radio Or Media Outlet Has A Connected Audience Or Has An Audience Interested In Your Music:

Not every radio station has the audience that they claim to. It's not necessarily that they are lying about how big their audience is, or how invested in the programming the listeners may be. But sometimes this is the case.

You don't just want radio airplay, because airplay to disengaged people doesn't bring you the results you want.

Remember why you're sending your music out there? You want to grow your fans and followers so that you can sell more music either on your website, at your concerts, or even in stores (brick-and-mortar as well as online). Disengaged audiences are less likely to pay attention to a new song, or the artist/band name attributed to it. This is why it's important for you to gauge how connected a station really is with its listener base.

There are a few ways you can gauge the connection, and some of these ways are very obvious. Spend some time on their social media platforms. Comments can be hard to come by for stations (and for businesses in general), but if a few posts are getting a Like or two, that's actually a really good sign.

From the time you spend on their website, see if they have images of their staff and any mention of involvement in the community. Look at the photos and images on the station/program's website. Images can be very telling because they give an indication of what the station/program wants to communicate to their listeners. A photo or image-rich site illustrates that the program or station wants to keep people on their site longer, and wants to interact with their listeners through engaging content. Their social media posts should do the same thing.

If you find yourself bored on a station's website, that can mean a few different things, and doesn't necessarily mean they have a disconnected audience. Web design may not be their strong suit or in their budget at the moment.

The station website and social media platforms should mention artists that they are keyed in on, or have featured in reviews and interviews. Notice the types of artists that these stations and programs are talking about. If they seem to be promoting a new release by a band in a very progressive rock style but also have a mention about a country or hip-hop band, that means they have a very eclectic programming format. You should key in on which hosts are more favorable to your style of music and try to reach out to them directly.

How to use radio promotion to land better gigs:
One good thing can create more good things. That's the nature of how success works. When you get added to one radio station, you can build on that success and be added to more. What helps you do this is a combination of things pertaining to how you market your music.

If you don't have an email newsletter, you should consider adding one. It's a great way to build the connection you seek with your individual fans, get them to attend your gigs, purchase your music directly from you, and get good feedback on what they like most about you. It's also a great way to tell them about the stations you're being heard on.

You should post on your social media channels the stations and programs that are playing your music. This is not only good karma and a great way to strengthen your connection with the radio outlets who are featuring you, but it illustrates that others are seeing the value in your music and promoting your work.

I mentioned that you can use radio promotion to coincide with touring. Your touring posts on social media and email should include mentioning the stations in the areas you're scheduled to play. When you can illustrate to venues that your music is being featured on radio and media outlets, as well as reviews from blogs, you are illustrating that you are a music entity with a growing following. Venues want to book bands that bring people into their space. Radio airplay is an indication of a growing band with an expanding audience base. Use your station adds when you contact venues.

One other mention about contacting venues, approach venues the same as you do with radio stations, because they are doing very similar things. Do your research. Make a new spreadsheet or list of venues you want to play at and look up what their booking policies are. Find out who the contact people are and send them an email. Tell them that you have a growing audience and that you average a range of X number of people at your shows. See if they will give you a slot to play with another band or if there is a process for getting in that will allow you to play for a cut of the door.

The radio airplay you receive can grow if you market yourself well. Add your station airplay to your EPK and website. State something along the lines of where your music is featured. Quote a line or two from reviews you've had. All of this benefits you when you put this info in front of other media outlets, booking agents, and promotions professionals.

Make sure you have taken in everything up to this point.

1. Why are non-commercial stations your best resource and option for radio promotion?

2. How important is it to build relationships instead of just putting your music in front of a radio manager?

3. Why should radio consider your music for feature on their platform?

4. What value do you add to the programming of indie and non-commercial radio?

5. What 5 stations do you want to get your music on because their audience is the people you most want to reach?

6. How can radio airplay help you land better gigs and concerts?

7. Why is it important to know whether or not to send a CD or digital music file to a station contact?

8. What type of audience are you wanting to reach with your music?

Chapter 10: Conclusion & Summary

Radio is a media outlet that creates and fosters connections with individuals. Your ability and opportunity to connect with these stations opens up the door for their audience to become yours as well.

I said early on that I would tell you my process for picking out music for a feature on my radio show, and what many stations and programs also use when going through their selection process. Here it is in a nutshell: We tend to sample various tracks from a new album or submission unless a specified track is listed for promotion on the submission.

The companies and radio promoters I mentioned typically will indicate which songs they are looking to get rotation for. This is a good starting point for artists who don't have a track record yet in terms of name recognition. This is why it is important for you to know the 1 or 2 best songs you are submitting so you can put those in front of the radio entity on the front end.

By sampling the music, I'm referring to giving it about 1-2 minutes listening. I'm listening for solid recording production (a polished sound that is EQ-ed and mastered), strong songwriting both lyrically and from a composition standpoint, and gauging how I feel about what I'm listening to.

Again, the listener experience is paramount to what gets the most (and best) feature on indie radio. When a song connects with me, I will want to showcase it to my audience.

When I find a submission that really sounds great, I will listen to more and more of it. If there are submissions that don't gel or hit the right way, I move on to the next submission.

Not everyone who submits gets a response back, usually because they don't do the followup to see where their music stands. When an artist contacts me for submission and addresses me or my program by name, I make more of a commitment to exploring their music, even giving honest feedback if it's not something that will be accepted. All of this is because the artist did the uncommon thing by addressing our show by name and asking a direct question. By showing me that you've had an experience with the platform I work on, you gain more favor than simply having a "cool song." The reason for this goes back to an earlier statement: you have to gain someone's favor and make a strong impression before people will give you consideration. If you can get someone to like you as a person by being genuine and uncommon, you gain so much more potential in them becoming not just a promotion platform but also a fan of your work.

Some good connections with artists and our brand, as well as other radio portals have come about from this line of communication.

The end result you want is a connection, so even if you don't get airplay the first time, if you can make a connection and exchange a few messages, good things have come from that endeavor.

Your ultimate goal is not airplay alone. Neither is it to sell out arenas or get your song heard on a TV show. All of those are great achievements and can provide great rewards for you. But they are pieces of the puzzle, and plateaus on the mountain climb to success. The end goal is sustained audience connection. Achieving a strong audience connection gives you the long-term success you can bank on and use to grow your music career.

What about Pandora, Spotify, or Apple Music? Won't getting on these platforms make me a successful artist?

As I mentioned in the first few sections of this book, Spotify, Pandora, and even Apple Music have provided for the music fans of the world an ongoing playlist of music that fits their individual interests. When mainstream and commercial radio turned in the 1970s and 80s and began only playing certain label's artists or certain popular artists, they set the stage for today's streaming technology to take the place in the realm of people who prefer select pop music on a regular basis.

Indie and unsigned artists can have their music heard on Spotify and Pandora and Apple Music and any other streaming service by submission process. However, similar to the myriad of bands and artists with Soundcloud, Reverbnation or similar sites, the sheer volume of artists with content is astounding.

It is very difficult to make traction on Spotify with a non-rotating playlist of artists (their setup is primarily through playlists from users) and musicians who are paired with other mainstream artists based on similar styles and era of music released.

Pandora's algorithm for programming and selecting artists for streaming is done through a ratings system. Songs and artists given positive ratings get heard more often that those with no rating or negative (thumbs down) ratings. Artists who have released music within certain eras or genre styles are associated together. For artists who can combine performance and other musical impressions on fans, they stand to gain much from being heard on Spotify and Pandora, as well as other media.

However, the mention earlier that music fans who only want to listen and not ever commit to supporting through music purchase or concerts are generally more prone to turn to Spotify or Pandora than indie radio. While it is important to get your music heard by as many people as you can in order to create more opportunities for fan conversion, relying only on Spotify or Pandora alone to achieve this will not result in the sustained audience growth you are looking for.

I encourage you to commit to the process of promotion, both through radio airplay as well as other forms of media broadcast including online reviews, podcast features, Spotify, and Pandora. There is not a one-size fits all solution to grow your music and gain the audience you want.

However, if you follow this handbook's direction, the growth and opportunities that will present themselves for you will give you the greatest opportunity for ongoing success that you can build on over time.

Best of luck to you, and please reach out to let me know how your journey is going. I encourage you to connect with me through my website http://dgrantsmith.com where I post regular tips, hints, podcast interviews with industry pros and leaders, and insights on how to grow your audience, connect with new fans, and reach your goals. Radio insights are a part of the offering there, and so much more.

You can reach out to me through email at dgrantsmith@gmail.com
I personally respond to every email message. As you have read, relationship connections are very important to me. I look forward to hearing from you and being a resource for you in growing your career. Thank you.

Take all of this to the next level and jump on the Indie Radio Course now, with your book discount at http://dgrantsmith.com/indieradiocourse-1handbookreaderdiscount25

About The Author

Smith presenting The Golden Fork Award to singer-songwriter Iron And Wine

D Grant Smith is an *award-winning host and creator of The Appetizer Radio Show, a weekly variety music program heard on radio stations across the country and around the world. Since 2003, he has worked with indie and unsigned musicians in growing their music fan base through airplay on indie radio outlets.
More information at http://appetizerradio.com

He also works as a coach and mentor to musicians in strategic fan growth and audience cultivation. Learn more at http://dgrantsmith.com

Smith lives in Texas with his wife and 2 cats. His musical interests include playing drums in some side bands including The Wonderful Land Wonderful Band and occasionally guitar. He also loves karaoke.

Smith enjoys stories, which is why he works with artists through radio and mentoring because of the opportunities to be a part of great stories. Aside from excellent and savory music, he enjoys craft beer, comic books, football, and boxing because in each of these, an amazing story is waiting to be told.

CPSIA information can be obtained
at www.ICGtesting.com
Printed in the USA
FSOW01n1834180516
20536FS